The Texas Cherokees

The Civilization of the American Indian Series

The Texas Cherokees

A People Between Two Fires 1819–1840

by Dianna Everett

University of Oklahoma Press : Norman and London

Library of Congress Cataloging-in-Publication Data

Everett, Dianna.
The Texas Cherokees : a people between two fires, 1819–1840 / Dianna Everett. — 1st ed.
p. cm. — (The Civilization of the American Indian series : v. 203)
Includes bibliographical references and index.
ISBN 0-8061-2296-X
1. Cherokee Indians—History—19th century. 2. Cherokee Indians—Government relations. 3. Indians of North America—Texas—History—19th century. I. Title. II. Series.
E99.C5E89 1990
976.4′004975—dc20 90-50233
CIP

The paper in this book meets the guidelines for permanence and durability of the Committee on Production Guidelines for Book Longevity of the Council on Library Resources, Inc. ♾

The Texas Cherokees: A People Between Two Fires, 1819–1840, is Volume 203 in The Civilization of the American Indian Series.

For Bobby and Robert

Contents

Illustrations

Maps

Preface

In 1839 a Texan general remarked to Chief Duwali, leader of the Texas Cherokees, that the Indians were "between two fires"; he referred to the position of the Texas troops, who at that moment flanked the Cherokees and prepared for battle. But the general's words took in a whole world of Cherokee experience, for these Indians had been "between two fires" since the advent of Europeans in North America. The Cherokees were troubled by the dichotomy between the ideal of harmony among individuals and the reality of factionalism in their everyday life, between the comfort of tradition and the practical necessity of accomodation to the ways of whites. They were caught between two fires in the struggle of European nations for the domination of a continent. They were caught between two fires in their emigration westward, with white settlers pressing in from the east while on the west other tribes resisted Cherokee emigration. The Cherokees met much the same situation in Texas, and at last, they found themselves between the two fires of removal and extermination. The story of the Texas Cherokees is the story of a people valiantly attempting to exercise self-determination in the face of a broader process which they were able to affect but not completely control.

The author wishes to express sincere gratitude to Seymour V. Connor, without whose urging this reinterpretation would not have been initiated, and to John R. Wunder, for skillfully guiding this project to fruition as a doctoral dissertation and for encouraging me to try to place the Texas Cherokees in ethnohistorical perspective rather than in the perspective of the political history of early Texas. Others who read the manuscript in its various stages and offered welcomed suggestions include Phil Dennis, Theda Perdue, Elizabeth John, and Mary E. Young.

I am also indebted to David Murrah and the staff of the Southwest Collection of Texas Tech University, for their valuable assistance in securing research materials, and to the staffs of the Texas State Archives, of the University of Texas's Eugene C. Barker Texas History Center, of the Oklahoma Historical Society Archives, and of the Thomas Gilcrease Institute of American History and Art, for opening their collections and for suggesting sources of useful information.

Finally, I wish to thank my husband, Bobby, and my son, Robert, whose encouragement over the past fourteen years is the principle reason this study has been completed.

DIANNA EVERETT

The Texas Cherokees

«»

1
The Cherokees Come to Texas

"I asked him, 'How do you live in that country?' He replied, 'We have good corn fields. We have plenty of cattle and hogs. We have plenty of Buffaloe and Deer. So that we soon can live better than we would have.' 'Do your women make any cloth?' 'Yes, they will never give up that'."—Kiamee, a Western Cherokee chief, in dialogue with R. J. Meigs, 6 April 1811 (Records of the Cherokee Agency in Tennessee, Roll 5, #2627).

In the monumental work *Myths of the Cherokees* ethnologist James Mooney relates a traditional tale of the "Lost Cherokees." Around the year 1721, as the story goes, a small part of the tribe, protesting against land cessions, left their homes to trek westward across the Mississippi. Because the wanderers never again communicated with their kinsmen in the east, their existence was only a dim memory when, years later, they were discovered by others of their tribe who were hunting at the base of the Rocky Mountains. The lost ones were living in an idyllic world similar to the Cherokee world before the advent of the European.[1]

Mooney's Cherokee informants recounted other strange tales of peoples who lived in the direction of the setting sun. "Guntsuskwali," or Short Arrows, as they called one society, could conceivably have been any number of Plains tribes whose bows and arrows differed from the weapons of woodland peoples such as the Cherokees. Storytellers also spoke of "Tsunilkalu," or slant-eyed people, and "Tsuniyatiga," or naked people, who also lived in the direction of the setting sun. Could the "Tsuniyatiga" have been Uto-Aztecan tribes of the Great Basin region? A more likely explanation is that the "Tsuniyatiga" were either Atakapans or Karankawas, both Texas coastal tribes whose members went about unclothed or semiclothed. "Yuniwinigiski," or man-eaters, may also have referred to Atakapans, Tonkawas, or Karankawas of Texas, all of whom reputedly practiced ceremonial cannibalism. Unfortunately, Mooney's informants did not elaborate further, and his versions of their tales leave so much to the imagination that the identity of these tribes cannot be firmly established. Nonetheless, the appearance of nominally "western" Indians in Cherokee folklore indicates that at an early date the Cherokees were interested in and may have been generally familiar with the inhabitants of parts of the trans-Mississippi West, perhaps even with Texas.[2]

The Cherokees call themselves "Ani-Yunwiya," the Principal People, and, indeed, they were one of the principal nations in the southeastern United States until their removal in the fourth decade of the nineteenth century. Of Iroquoian linguistic stock, in pre-Columbian times Cherokees had occupied the region about the headwaters of the Ohio River until the Iroquois and Delawares drove them southward.[3] A Cherokee migration legend, recited in early times during ceremonies, tells of the tribe's creation in a land lying in the direction of the rising sun, where they lived amidst snakes and water monsters. From this homeland, according to the legend, they migrated toward present-day Virginia.[4]

Historians and archeologists have established the plausibility of this legend, at least in terms of the reality of a migration. Under pressure from northern peoples, over several centuries the tribe drifted into the Appalachian highlands, where they came to occupy present-day western North Carolina, western South Carolina, northern Georgia, northeastern Alabama, and eastern Tennessee.[5] By 1000 A.D. they were participating in the development and decline of a complex culture, called Mississippian, which they shared with the Choctaws, the Chickasaws, the Creeks, the Natchez, such other southeastern groups as the Kadohadachos, and other tribes of eastern Texas.[6] By the midsixteenth century Cherokees lived as sedentary agriculturalists, and their elaborate social, political, and ceremonial structures were fairly representative of the tribes of the southeastern culture area.[7]

In 1540, when they first saw Europeans, the Cherokees may have numbered as many as 16,000, living in four distinct regional settlement areas scattered through 100,000 square miles.[8] Their first encounter with Europeans came in 1540 when members of a Spanish expedition led by Hernando de Soto camped along the Keowee River in present-day South Carolina.[9] Subsequently, for the next two centuries, economic expansionism and colonization of North America by the English, French, and Spanish placed pressure on all native peoples for trade, for military alliances, and for territorial concessions.

All the while, contact with men and women of these nations, as well as with American-born colonials, influenced the Cherokees' lives in many ways, producing phenomenal changes in the native culture. An interesting aspect of Cherokee society in pre-Columbian and colonial times was its flexibility and traditional openness to change. New and useful material objects, new people, and, to some extent, new ideas, had always been included and adapted to fit Cherokee ways. Through constant contact with colonists of various nationalities, the Cherokees learned much about Europeans and about how to deal with their peculiar customs and ideas. By virtue of their involvement in the fur trade after 1673, the Cherokees obtained and adapted many material elements of European culture, intermarried with Europeans, and adopted them into their tribe. All during the eighteenth century, as a consequence of the lengthy and sometimes brutal process of European empire building, the Principal People suffered calamitous wars, epidemics, and food shortages, always resulting in shrinking population, shrinking territory, and fractioning of group identity.[10]

As colonial competition and wars dragged on throughout the eighteenth century, the Cherokees were seldom able to present a united front before the enemy. In traditional Cherokee culture, harmony of persons with nature and of individual with individual was an important social ideal, one which had always functioned to minimize interpersonal strife.[11] In reality, however, an outstanding characteristic of Cherokee life was factionalism in political and diplomatic affairs. A century of war had exacerbated the tendency, making the Cherokees more aggressive toward their external enemies and more contentious among themselves. Factions had always existed to allow the airing of divergent opinions before a consensus could be reached and unified action taken; this was no less true in the colonial era than in years before.[12] Factionalism surfaced often in response to social dislocation, but now factions arose to dispute land cessions and to engage in unauthorized diplomatic negotiations with various rival European nations.[13] In these decades Cherokee diplomacy was characterized by a tendency for various chiefs or regions to negotiate independently to sell their services, in trade or alliances, to the nation offering the most advantage. Often these alliances were temporary and brought destruction to the Indian community. Despite their valiant efforts, by 1791 the Cherokees were defeated militarily and were virtually subjugated to the authority of a nascent United States government, which quickly set in motion a program of promoting the tribe's acculturation to "civilized" ways.

By a treaty made with the United States in 1791, the Cherokees were to be provided with "implements of husbandry" and other manufactured goods on an annual basis.[14] Demoralized and disorganized, too tired to fight any longer, many Cherokees set out upon a treacherous path toward "civilization," as U.S. officials called it. Rapidly acquiring material possessions through trade and influence, many men and women adapted the outward trappings of Western material culture. After 1794 Indian agents pressed many Cherokees into adopting more intensive farming as a primary means of subsistence. This led to a dispersal of people out from the villages and onto individual farmsteads. In turn, the young had fewer contacts with the elderly, the keepers and teachers of tradition, and there was a concomitant decline in communal and ceremonial life. All of this was possible largely because of the flexibility of the Cherokee social system. In the early decades of the nineteenth century the outward appearances of traditional Cherokee culture began to disappear except

Sketch of Duwali, leader of the Texas Cherokees, drawn by William A. Berry, from contemporary descriptions. Used by permission of the Jenkins Company, Austin, Texas; photo courtesy Texas State Library, Austin, Texas.

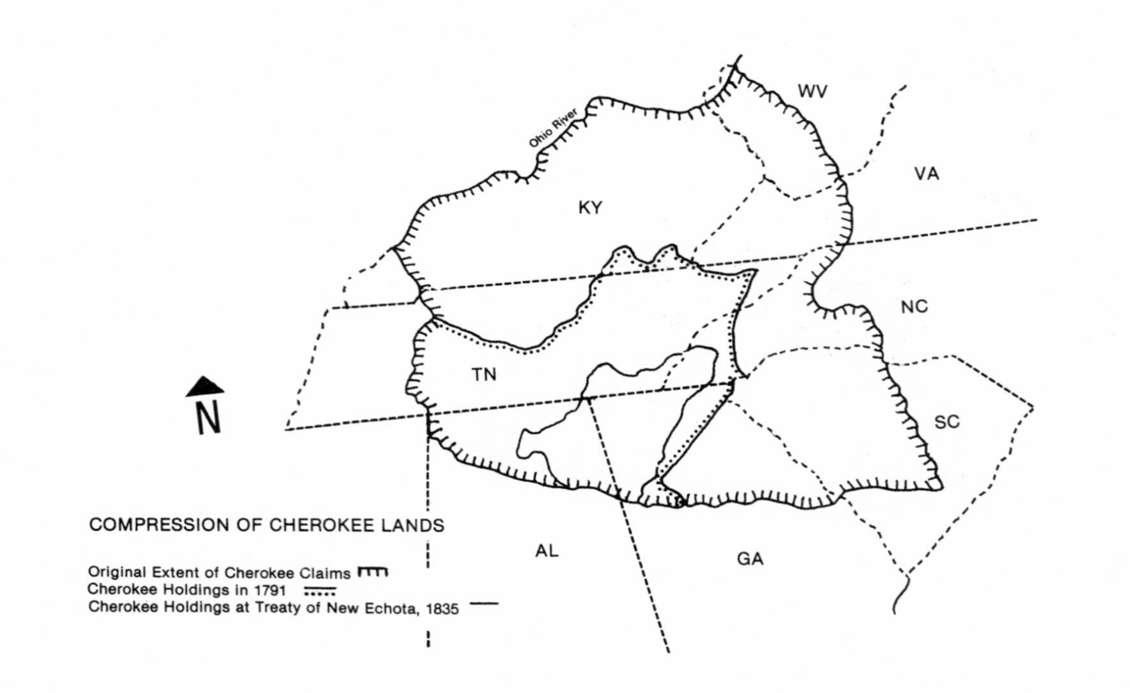

COMPRESSION OF CHEROKEE LANDS

among the most conservative and the most impoverished; nevertheless, many clung, at least in spirit, to traditional attitudes and beliefs.[15] By 1820 Cherokee society east of the Mississippi, under the guidance of Indian agents and a cadre of mixed-blood leaders, was beginning to resemble, at least superficially, the culture of the American South.

From 1794 to 1810 factional disputes, still functional in intratribal politics, were exacerbated by the continuing pressure of internal social change and by the continuing pressure of the U.S. government for additional land cessions. Three major factions developed: one favored tribal unity, centralized government, and an end to cessions; a second favored a formal division of the nation into constituent factions; and a third favored land cessions and removal west of the Mississippi. This debate over land cessions was one important factor propelling Cherokees westward to Arkansas and Texas in the early years of the century. Traditionally, in cases of irreconcilable difference, one or another faction (usually the minority) was free to withdraw and live elsewhere so that consensus could prevail (at least temporarily) within the group.[16] From 1791 to 1820 thousands of dissidents and traditionalists withdrew in true Cherokee fashion, crossed the Great River, and preserved what remained of traditional lifeways in a new world.

For many reasons Cherokees found the trans-Mississippi country attractive. Much of the river's western drainage resembled the tribe's homelands in Tennessee and the Carolinas. In present-day eastern Arkansas and southeastern Missouri were lowlands suitable for trapping, gathering, and farming. The Ozark highlands of present-day southern Missouri and northwestern Arkansas resembled the Appalachian highlands, harboring herds of deer and thousands of beaver, otter, and other animals prized by Cherokee trappers and traders. On the edge of the plains, in present-day eastern Oklahoma and southeastern Kansas, and perhaps even as far south and west as Texas, the Cherokees could hope to roam free, profiting from the winter hunt, raising their children in traditional ways, and maintaining harmony, free from internecine strife.

Cherokee use of western lands had begun in the second half of the eighteenth century. Because of increasing reliance on the fur trade by Cherokees and other tribes, game had become scarce east of the Mississippi as the eighteenth century wore on. The Cherokees returned winter after winter to trans-Mississippi hunting grounds. At least as early as the 1770s, Cherokee hunting parties are known to have camped and followed herds of deer in the valleys and along the tributaries of the St. Francis, White, and Arkansas rivers in Spanish Louisiana.[17] Some of the headmen recognized the practicality of moving their entire operation, village and all, across the river. In 1788 a Cherokee headman named Toquo, or Turkey, petitioned Don Manuel Perez, residing in St. Louis as governor of Spanish Illinois, to ". . . grant him the favor of giving refuge to his whole nation in the territory of the great king of Spain."[18] Although Spanish officials feared a mass movement of Indians to the west, Esteban Miró, commandant general of Louisiana, nevertheless approved the emigration of up to six villages.[19]

Cherokees then settled in the valley of the St. Francis River, a fertile region in present-day Missouri and Arkansas where soil was suitable for growing corn, hemp, and other crops. Throughout the last decade of the eighteenth century, Cherokee headmen sought and received permission to settle there; at least two large communities were established.[20] In 1804, after the 1803 Louisiana Purchase was made by the United States, Meriwether Lewis, leading the first U.S. expedition into the newly acquired territory, observed that two large Cherokees towns located on the St. Francis River could raise 250 warriors.[21] In 1807 and 1808, a trickle became a flood because of a resettlement policy inaugurated by President Thomas Jefferson.[22] This presented an opportunity for Cherokees to escape social change and factional disputes and to maintain war and hunting practices by withdrawing and moving west.

In the early months of 1810 several prominent chiefs led large emigrant parties down the Tennessee River and across the Mississippi. In January, Duwali, also known as Bowl and Bold Hunter, chief of the town of Little Hiwasee (in present-day western North Carolina, on the Hiwassee River), and another headman, named Saulowee (Tsulawi, or Fox), jointly conducted a group of seventy-five from their villages.[23] In February, Talontuskee, another prominent chief, led a large party to the St. Francis; soon after his arrival, Talontuskee became nominal leader of all of the "Western" Cherokees.[24] Subsequently, the Cherokee National Council condemned these emigrants as traitors for accepting the U.S. government's offer and for moving west without the consent of the Cherokee nation. Duwali's and Takatoka's people settled along the White and St. Francis rivers in present-day northeastern Arkansas; a few other emigrant parties went immediately to the Arkansas River, settling on both the north and the south bank. This wave of settlement increased the Western Cherokee population to approximately two thousand.[25] From their towns these Western Cherokees roamed westward and southward, raiding, hunting, and trading in Arkansas, Louisiana, and Texas. Within the decade, Duwali's followers would move on to Spanish Texas.

The first report of Cherokees visiting Spanish Texas came in 1807. In March of that year, a party of hunters traveled down the Red River to Natchitoches, Louisiana, where the United States had recently built a trading factory. According to Dr. John Sibley, the Indian agent, these Cherokees, the first of their people ever to visit his post, brought deerskins to trade. The party identified their home as a village higher up on the waterway; this constitutes the first report of Cherokees on or near the Red River.[26] Their presence so far south of the Arkansas settlements indicates that an expanding Cherokee population there may have been forcing Cherokees to seek trade elsewhere.

Three months later, in August, a delegation of immigrant Indians, led by a Pascagoula chief called Pinayé, arrived in Nacogdoches, the easternmost Spanish town in Texas. Presenting himself to Captain Francisco Viana, commandant of the local troops, Pinayé claimed to represent the Pascagoulas, a southeastern tribe originally from Mississippi but then resident in southeastern Louisiana,[27] as well as a number of villages of Cherokees, Chickasaws, and Shawnees. The chief sought permission to settle members of those tribes in Texas.

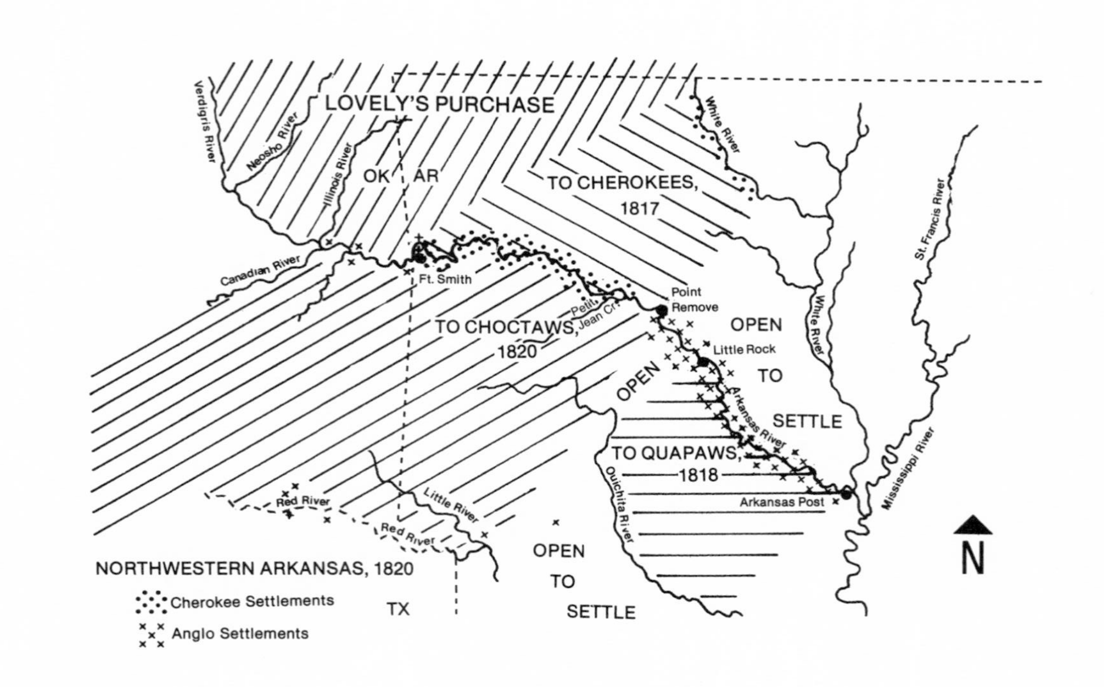

NORTHWESTERN ARKANSAS, 1820

The request moved through the Spanish bureaucracy, as Viana forwarded the request to Antonio Cordéro, governor of Texas, who in turn forwarded it to his superior, Nemesio Salcedo, commandant general of Spain's Internal Provinces. Salcedo tentatively approved the "transfer into these territories [Texas] by the parties of Pascagoulas, Chickasaws, Cherokees, and Shawnees which have solicited inspection and were given account of in your official communication of September 4."[28]

Pinayé's claim to represent segments of several different tribes may have been based on the presence of emigrants from these peoples who had come into the Arkansas-Missouri-Louisiana region in the first decade of the century. Among the Cherokees it was traditional to send delegations to conduct diplomatic matters; therefore, he may have been representing them. Although none are mentioned, Cherokees probably accompanied the Pascagoulas to Nacogdoches. The granting of Pinayé's request was also consonant with Spanish policy and practice, under which immigrant U.S. Indians had been admitted in 1783 and 1788 as a buffer against American expansion into territory west of the Mississippi.[29]

Following this, Cherokees drifted into and out of Louisiana and Texas. In 1813 members of a filibustering expedition led into Texas by Bernardo Gutiérrez de Lara and Augustus W. Magee found several families, whom they thought to be Cherokees, encamped in Texas on the Trinity River fifty or sixty miles south of Nacogdoches.[30] In 1816 John Jamison, Dr. Sibley's successor as agent at the Natchitoches factory, reported that one hundred Cherokees resided within his superintendency. In April 1817 Jamison accompanied a military party up the Red River and reported villages of Cherokees and Delawares on the east bank several miles south of present-day Fulton, Arkansas, where the Little River joins the Red.[31] Jamison's observations were corroborated by Colonel William A. Trimble, commanding the Eighth Regiment of the U.S. Army in Arkansas. In 1817, while in charge of the western portion of the Eighth Military Department, Trimble had gathered information on the Indian tribes of Arkansas, Louisiana, and Texas. In his investigation Trimble ascertained that the "Coushattas, Delawares, and Cherokees obtained permission from the

Caddos to settle on the Red River." He added that the Cherokees "do not claim part of the country. . . . The Cherokees came, within the last few years, from the Arkansaw [*sic*]."[32]

On the Arkansas River, where the majority of the Western Cherokees resided, population pressures worked to engender a southerly migration which would soon carry more Cherokees into Spanish territory. By the terms of a treaty made in 1817, the Western Cherokees had agreed to give up their claim to land rights in the east in exchange for a permanent reserve in northern Arkansas; and the Eastern Cherokees agreed to cede their claim to territory in Tennessee and South Carolina. The Cherokees living on the south bank of the Arkansas were to move north to be inside the reserve. The United States promised to assist Cherokees in moving west, and soon hundreds began emigrating; by 1819 the Western Cherokee population had climbed to more than 3,000.[33] In the years between 1812, when Missouri Territory was created, and 1819, when Arkansas Territory was separated from Missouri, several thousand American frontiersmen moved into Arkansas County, the southwestern portion of Missouri Territory. Within a brief time the American population established farms along both banks of the Arkansas River from Arkansas Post past Point Remove, at the southeast corner of the Cherokee reserve.[34] By 1821 the American population was approaching three thousand,[35] and the valley of the Arkansas had become a patchwork of tribal reserves, open settlement areas, and public lands closed to settlement.

As population pressure mounted due to American and Cherokee emigration, Western Cherokee leaders struggled to preserve access to hunting areas west of their reserve. This region, called "Lovely's Purchase," was also used by the Osages, who had become enemies of the Cherokees when the latter began crossing the Mississippi at the turn of the century. In 1818 the Osages ceded the region to the United States.[36] Subsequently, Secretary of War John C. Calhoun decided to offer this newly acquired land to the Cherokees in exchange for Cherokee land cessions east of the Mississippi.[37] Treaties and concessions notwithstanding, the Cherokees still had to contend with the Osages for use of the area as a hunting ground. Among Western Cherokee leaders there was a definite lack of consensus on how to deal with the Osages. Takatoka, nominally war chief, and Duwali, a village headman, led a faction determined to maintain the tradition of war and revenge. John Jolly, who in 1817 succeeded his brother Talontuskee as principal chief, led the majority in supporting a plan of diplomatic negotiations with the enemy in order to preserve Cherokee lives and property.[38]

The search for consensus was to be difficult, for the argument lay rooted in a basic principle of Cherokee social structure: enforcement of the rule of vengeance. This was one of the most important functions of Cherokee kin groups, the clans.[39] The rule of vengeance operated to maintain social order within the community and also operated in intertribal warfare: clan members were expected to avenge a kinsman's death caused by a member of another tribe; in this case, deaths caused by the Osages must be avenged. In the East, among the more acculturated Cherokees, this principle was generally ignored, although some still clandestinely followed the rule. In fact, the government of the Eastern Cherokees had abolished it in 1810.[40] But the principle was still strongly at work on the frontier among the Western Cherokees, who could not reach a consensus on the question. Takatoka upheld the principle, adamantly refused to attend John Jolly's peace conferences, and openly urged Duwali and other headmen to pursue revenge whenever necessary.[41] Raids and counter-raids were frequent in 1818 and 1819, despite the peace party's efforts. In mid-1819 the Osages dispatched three Cherokee hunters in one raid; later, in council, Duwali, publicly argued in favor of retaliation and announced that he would not support a consensus for negotiation.[42] His position was unpopular with the Western Cherokees' council, who were at the moment considering a resolution to outlaw clan revenge.[43] The dissenters' continuing withdrawal from the consensus signalled a new migration of traditionalists away from a center of change.

The withdrawal principle was made manifest in emigration southward. In April 1819 a prominent chief told Thomas Nuttall, a naturalist touring the Cherokee country, that he intended to "proceed across Red River and petition land from the Spaniards."[44] In the spring and summer many Cherokees, as well as Delawares, Creeks, and Choctaws, entered and settled in Lost Prairie, an area between the Sulphur Fork and the Red River. The Cherokee village earlier established near present Fulton, Arkansas, continued to grow, as well.[45] In the winter of 1819–1820 other villages, including perhaps Duwali's, moved southward to Lost Prairie.[46] These included both Cherokee traditionalists and those residents on the south bank of the Arkansas River who had refused the request to move north onto the reserve. By the spring of 1820 there were at least two hundred Cherokees, in addition to several hundred Delawares, Chickasaws, and Choctaws, residing near the Great Bend of the river.[47]

The haven to which the Cherokees and other displaced southeastern Indians were drawn lay in extreme southwestern Arkansas, where the Red River changes its direction of flow from eastward to southward. On either side of the river were broad expanses of prairie: on the east and north lay Mound Prairie; Long or Lost Prairie nestled on the south and west bank of the river.[48] The fertile valley of the Red River between present-day Texas, Oklahoma, and Arkansas had been the home of the Kadohadacho, one of the largest tribes of the Caddo confederacy. Although many of their villages had been located in the Great Bend, by the early 1800s the Kadohadacho population had been depleted by epidemics and by Osage attacks. The tribe had retreated into Texas and also down the Red River into southwestern Louisiana, leaving the Lost Prairie area open.[49] The prairie expanse and surrounding forests provided good hunting, grazing, and farming for the new arrivals, and the Red River provided an avenue of transportation to the Sulphur Fork and Natchitoches factories.

Through the center of the Great Bend region lay Trammel's Trace, a trail leading from Missouri across Arkansas and into Texas. This well-traveled thoroughfare was a major avenue of entry into Texas for Indians and settlers alike. The route passed near present-day Hot Springs, Washington, and Fulton, Arkansas. Crossing the Red River and the Sulphur Fork, or South

Little River, the trail led through the present site of Jefferson, Texas, southward to Nacogdoches.[50]

Joining the Cherokees, Delawares, and other tribes in the race to occupy the region lying between the Arkansas and Red rivers were Americans. At least seven settlements had been made in or near the valley of the Red River by 1820, despite the recognized claim of the Quapaws and, later, of the Choctaws to the land. As early as 1811 settlers had begun gathering on the south side of the Red River at Pecan Point in present Red River County, Texas, then in Spanish territory.[51] Between 1815 and 1820 villages and trading posts were established at Pecan Point, on the Red; at Jonesborough, on the south side of the river upstream from Pecan Point; at the mouth of the Kiametia River; at Mound Prairie, near present-day Washington, Arkansas; and at present-day Fulton, where the main Little River joins the Red.[52] Although the U.S. government repeatedly tried to remove some of the settlers, by late 1820 the American population numbered in the thousands.[53]

In the years during which both Cherokees and Anglos were moving into territory in and adjacent to present-day Texas, the boundary between the United States and Spanish Texas remained indistinct and undefined. In 1803, when the United States purchased Louisiana, American and French commissioners had not delineated the western boundary of Louisiana. In 1806 Spanish and American officials had negotiated an agreement creating a Neutral Ground or "no-man's-land" between southern Texas and southern Louisiana. The Neutral Ground was bounded on the east by a line drawn from Bayou Pierre (near present-day Coushatta, Louisiana) southward to the Calcasieu River and down that stream to the Gulf. The western boundary was the Sabine River, and the northern border was set by a line drawn from Sabine to Bayou Pierre. According to the agreement, all Americans were to remain east of the buffer zone, and all Spaniards were to curtail their activities east of the Sabine. The Neutral Ground became a haven for individual outcasts from both nations, as well as an avenue of entry for Chickasaws, Choctaws, and several other tribes moving into southeastern Texas.[54] Further north, above the zone, the Red River seems generally to have been accepted as the international border. Most Americans who settled in and around the Great Bend remained on the east and north bank, and the dissident Cherokees crossed over to the west and south bank.

In 1819 Spain and the United States settled the boundary question. In the Adams-Onís Treaty, concluded in February, the United States renounced its claim to Texas, and the western limits of the Louisiana Purchase were defined, on paper at least, leaving the Lost Prairie area within the boundary of the United States.[55] Not until 1821 did Spain ratify the treaty, and the boundary remained indistinct until Texas became a part of the United States.

During 1818, 1819, and 1820 life in Lost Prairie assumed a nightmarish quality for the Cherokees and other tribes. Many of their American neighbors were part-time traders, who purveyed whiskey to the Indians for four to six dollars per gallon and bartered trinkets for furs and skins. In the village near present-day Fulton, Arkansas, Cherokee leaders complained to Jacob Fowler, Indian agent at the Sulphur Fork factory, that they had "no order or subordination in their village and very little control over their men, and since the whites have come among them with great quantities of whiskey they have all become very poor and miserable."[56] Fowler advised Superintendent of Indian Trade Thomas A. McKinney to break up the American settlements because the traders were cheating the Indians and encouraging depletion of the game supply.[57] Several traders had been allowed to move into the village, but in the spring of 1819 they were summarily ejected when one bludgeoned a Cherokee man, "a half-Blood Cherokee who could read and write a good hand," and frightened him into returning to the Arkansas River.[58] In December this entire village packed up and moved across the Red River, settling on the west bank in territory presumed by their leaders to be Spanish.[59]

Cherokees who were in the process of moving from the Arkansas to the Red River were also encountering difficulties. Many came to the Sulphur Fork factory to trade, and in the opinion of Agent Fowler they were "dissatisfied, and entirely undetermined about a future settlement—they hunt very little and are generally destitute of almost every necessity."[60] Close proximity to American farmers in and around Lost Prairie tempted impoverished Cherokee hunters to expropriate the settlers' cattle and other commodities. In April 1820 the citizens of Hempstead County, writing to Arkansas Governor James Miller, recited a familiar litany of offenses allegedly committed since 1817 by Cherokees, Osages, Caddoes, and assorted "strolling bands" of Indians in Lost Prairie.[61] In May another citizens' group alleged that Bowl (Duwali), Hog-in-the-Pen, and other Cherokees living west of the Red River had recently stolen horses from a resident of Pecan Point. The settlers demanded that the governor remove the Cherokees and send them back to the Arkansas River.[62]

Informed of the alleged crimes, a council of Western Cherokee chiefs condemned the wanderers as individuals who refused to be governed. The leaders disclaimed responsibility for their actions.[63] The Western Cherokees were in the process of creating a government at this time, and it appears that they would no longer brook "withdrawals" from group decisions and rules.[64] For the Cherokees in Lost Prairie, however, life became increasingly desperate and chaotic, and they began to consider moving further into Spanish territory.

In 1820 east Texas offered a haven for the homeless, hardy, adventurous Indian or frontiersman. A land of rolling hills and many streams, its topography, climate, and vegetation was an extension of the forested southeastern United States.[65] Pines and hardwoods abounded, the river valleys were fertile, and game was still plentiful. In the years preceding the arrival of the Western Cherokees, Caddoan and Wichitan tribes had inhabited the region.

From earliest times through the mideighteenth century Caddoan-speaking tribes had predominated in eastern Texas. The Caddoans were sedentary agriculturalists who built large permanent villages. Their complicated kinship, ceremonial, and political configurations were typical of southeastern culture groups. Over a dozen tribes had belonged to one or another Caddoan confederacy. Four tribes of the Kadohadacho confederacy had lived along the Red River in present Texas

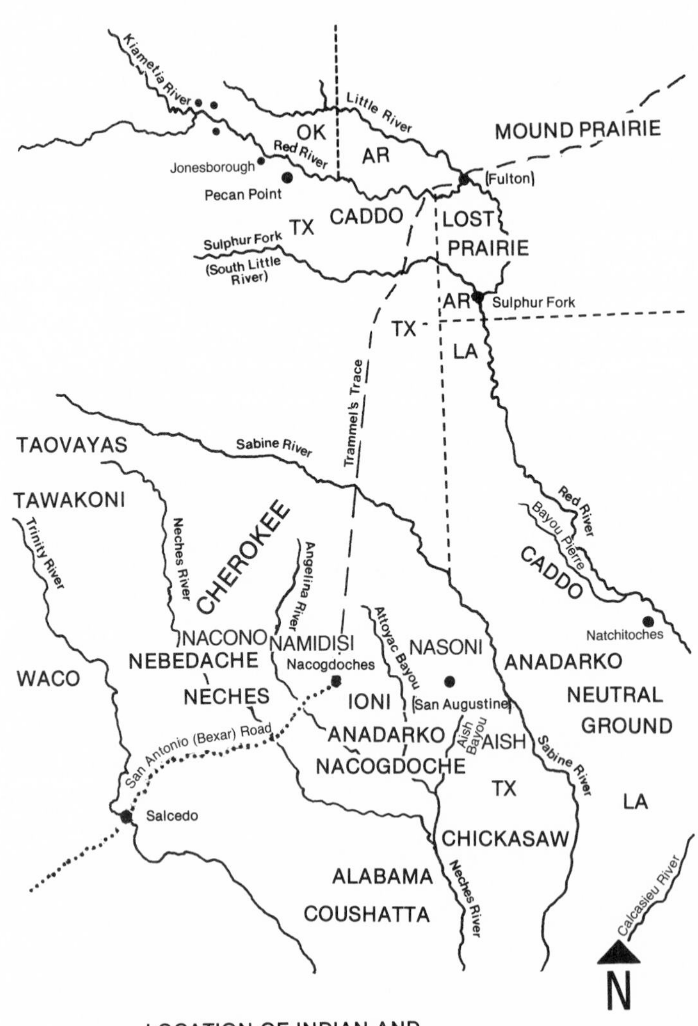

LOCATION OF INDIAN AND
SPANISH SETTLEMENTS IN EAST TEXAS, 1820

and Louisiana. Eight tribes of the Hasinai confederacy had lived along the tributaries and in the valleys of the Angelina and Neches rivers. The Hasinai tribes had been the objects of Spanish missionary fervor in the late seventeenth and early eighteenth centuries. In fact, the first Spanish settlements in Texas had been made by missionaries working with these tribes.[66]

By the opening of the nineteenth century, however, only vestiges of the Caddoan confederacies remained. Their demise was due primarily to epidemics that carried off thousands of Indians at a time. Along the Red River, between Texas and present-day Oklahoma, were a few small villages of Kadohadachos. Hasinai tribes lived further south: on the Sabine River, near Spanish Lagoon, were villages of Anadarkos; on the branches of the Angelina River, east of the small Spanish community of Nacogdoches, were villages of Anadarkos, Nasonis, Nacogdoches, Ionis (Hainais), and Namidisi; to the west on the Neches River were villages of Nebedaches, Naconos, and Neches. The Aish, another Caddoan group, lived east of Nacogdoches on Attoyac Bayou.[67] Once numbering tens of thousands, by 1820 the Caddoes numbered no more than two thousand.[68]

Further westward, between the Brazos and Trinity rivers, were villages of Wacos, Tawakonis, and Taovayas, all of whom were Wichitan-speaking tribes. In precontact centuries Wichitans had led sedentary lives as agriculturalists. After the introduction of the horse in the early eighteenth century, however, they gradually adopted a semisedentary existence, abandoning their villages during the winter hunt and rebuilding and planting crops each spring. The Wichitan tribes were noted for aggressive diplomacy and prowess in war. In 1820 the Wacos, Tawakonis, and Taovayas may have numbered as many as two thousand.[69]

On the plains west of these tribes roamed bands of Comanches. These nomadic people were excellent horsemen, extremely mobile, and generally predisposed by their culture to expansionism. By the 1820s Comanche warriors were engaging in conflicts with the Americans and Spaniards and with indigenous and immigrant Indians in east Texas.[70]

Several other southeastern tribes normally resident east of the Mississippi had preceded the Cherokees into east Texas. At an indeterminate point in time between 1806 and 1819 a portion of the Alabamas had settled approximately sixty miles south of Nacogdoches on the Neches River.[71] Originally from the state of the same name, the Alabamas had migrated through Mississippi into the Neutral Ground of Louisiana during the eighteenth century. Similarly, a portion of the Coushatta tribe had migrated from Alabama through Mississippi and Louisiana into Texas. In the first decade of the century several hundred had settled on the Neches and Trinity rivers south of Nacogdoches.[72] In addition, a number of Choctaws had settled on the Sabine and lower Neches by 1814, and a small village of Chickasaws settled at the junction of the Neches and Angelina at the same time.[73]

One of New Spain's eight northern provinces, Texas in 1820 was sparsely populated, and east Texas was practically devoid of Spanish population. North of San Antonio only three communities existed. The largest, Nacogdoches, originally had been the site of an early eighteenth-century Spanish Indian mission. The area had been resettled in 1771, and by 1820 the community had grown into the second largest town in Texas. Ayish Bayou, near present-day San Augustine, had also been the site of an early mission; briefly settled again in 1794, it was occupied by Americans in the early years of the nineteenth century. In 1805 Santísima Trinidad de Salcedo, known as Trinidad, had been established at the Trinity River crossing of a road leading from San Antonio to Nacogdoches. North of Ayish Bayou and Nacogdoches and south of Pecan Point and Jonesborough there was no settlement. Although the land was inviting, it remained vacant because of filibustering activity by the Magee-Gutiérrez expedition of 1812–1813, which used the region as a corridor for an invasion of Texas. Although the filibusterers nearly succeeded in capturing Texas, they eventually faltered in their purposes; but their activities in east Texas frightened away most of the Spanish inhabitants. When the expedition's cohorts were routed in 1813, they retired to the Neutral Ground of Louisiana, and their proximity to east Texas intimidated all but the most intrepid settlers.[74] By 1820 the entire white population of the eastern half of the province of Texas probably numbered fewer than one thousand.[75] The region of Texas adjacent to Arkansas and Louisiana was a prime target for immigration both by displaced southeastern Indians and by American frontiersmen. There were few indigenous inhabitants, and there were even fewer Spanish settlers to block the path of such newcomers as the Cherokees.

Thus, over the winter of 1819–1820, the first Cherokees known to have settled permanently in Texas crossed the Red River into presumed Spanish territory. The leader of this group was probably Duwali, already mentioned as a prominent, if somewhat infamous, Western Cherokee chief. Many years later Duwali recalled that he had led his people from their village on Petit Jean Creek, near the Arkansas River, to a new home in Lost Prairie. After planting and harvesting a crop near the Red River, in the winter of 1820–1821 he and his followers had relocated their village further westward, at the Three Forks of the Trinity River. They remained on the Trinity for perhaps one planting season and one hunting season; they moved on, according to the chief, because they were constantly at war with the Taovayas over hunting rights.[76] At an undetermined point in late 1821 or early 1822, during the winter hunting season, Duwali's people moved eastward into the uninhabited region north of Nacogdoches, and others of the tribe soon followed their example.

«»

2
"What Is to Be Done with Us Poor Indians?"

"I am a Red man and a man of honor and cant be imposed on this way We will lift up our tomahawks and fight for land with all those friendly tribes that wishes land also If I am beaton, I then will Resign to fate and if not I will hold lands By the forse of my Red Warriors.—Richard Fields, December 1826 (Peter Ellis Bean to Stephen F. Austin, 31 December 1826, in Barker, ed., Austin Papers *1:1553).*

Duwali and other chiefs led their followers deep into the east Texas woods and set about building homes, clearing underbrush, breaking ground in the old Caddo fields, planting crops, making initial contacts with other immigrant tribes, and scouting the locations of indigenous peoples. For the ensuing twenty years the Texas Cherokees, along with bands from other southeastern tribes, made a stand in east Texas. For the first decade, at least, the Mexican government welcomed their presence as a buffer against an advancing American frontier. Most of the Cherokees cleared land and carved out farms in the uninhabited region directly north of Nacogdoches, on the upper branches of the Neches, Angelina, and Sabine rivers. By 1822 their population had grown to nearly three hundred.[1]

In some ways, the Cherokees' future in Texas was destined to be different from their existence in Arkansas. They would find new enemies in the Comanches, whose nomadic ways and loose political organization would frustrate Cherokee political plans. They would be forced to deal with a new "host" government; quite unlike the government of the United States, the government of Mexico was unstable and its policies were inconsistent, due primarily to frequent changes in administration. On the other hand, the Cherokees would find some uncomfortably familiar situations in Texas. Warfare with Comanches would replace warfare with Osages, and Cherokees would make defensive and offensive alliances with other southeastern tribes, both immigrant and indigenous. Furthermore, in a few years the steadily westward-moving American frontier would catch up with them, and they would spend much energy warding off encroachments. Finally, they would once again find themselves negotiating to preserve their new homes from preemption.

But for three years south of the Red River, from 1821 to 1824, Duwali's people remained for the most part undisturbed by the spectres of frontier expansion and intertribal conflict which had motivated Cherokees to emigrate westward to Arkansas and southward to Texas. Apparently, during these years Cherokee headmen had become conditioned to accept the necessity of holding legal title to real property. The chiefs realized that their future in Texas might well depend upon securing a treaty or guarantee from a non-Indian sovereignty. Therefore, for the first few years of the 1820s chiefs of the Texas Cherokees made concerted efforts to persuade Mexican authorities to give them a land grant in east Texas.

Texas's provincial officials at first took scant notice of the arrival of immigrant Indians. In April 1821 Antonio Martínez, Spanish governor of the Province of Texas, acknowledged that a large number of Cherokees, Choctaws, Miamis, and Kickapoos had been allowed to establish themselves in Texas. Overestimating the tribes' combined fighting strength at twenty-five thousand warriors, the governor recommended that these newcomers be "established in the country of the Comanches" where they could form a barrier between bands of that tribe and the east Texas settlements.[2] In September 1821 Mexico gained independence from Spain; in November a junta ruling Mexico, under the leadership of Agustín de Iturbide, expressed its good intentions toward the "Northern Indians."[3] For the Cherokees, the time appeared to be right for opening diplomatic negotiations with Mexico, and in early 1822 Richard

Fields, the Texas Cherokees' chief diplomat, began corresponding with Mexican authorities.

Richard Fields, one-eighth Cherokee, born in 1780, had first appeared in a public role in 1801 as liaison between the Cherokee tribal council and the U.S. agency in Tennessee.[4] In 1812 he had served as an interpreter in a treaty between the Chickasaws and Creeks, and in 1814 during the Creek War he had served as a captain of Cherokee Auxiliaries attached to General Andrew Jackson's army.[5] In 1822, still a relatively young and vigorous man, he came to serve as the premier diplomatic representative of the Western Cherokees in Texas, a post he continued to hold until his death in 1827. Talented, knowledgeable, and experienced, Fields was well qualified for the arduous task of securing a land grant for his people.

Fields's selection for this important mission, in all probability approved by consensus in an intervillage council at Duwali's village, reveals that traditional political organization and methods of conducting diplomacy were still operative in the early nineteenth century, at least among the Texas Cherokees. In early historic times the Cherokees had been organized into chiefdoms, with each village an independent political community; in later historic times, this tradition had continued, but with each village sending one or more representatives to an intervillage council. Within each chiefdom, as within a community of villages, a division of duties was standard. A "white," or political, organization functioned during peacetime; it was composed of a council of elders, called "beloved men," of which the foremost, either in terms of age or respect, was nominally "white chief" or "uku." Among the Texas Cherokees, this post was held by Duwali, whose age of sixty-two in 1822, as well as his accomplishments, fitted him for the duty. A "red" organization operated when the council voted to make war or conduct negotiations. The "red" organization also handled diplomatic missions. In the nineteenth century diplomats were primarily war chiefs, men from the age category of mature warriors. Missions to conduct negotiations for peace, war, and diplomatic agreements were still handled by members of the war organization.[6] Richard Fields was not civil leader of the Western Cherokees in Texas, as has been assumed by chroniclers of his career; his talents lay in the diplomatic field, and, in traditional Cherokee fashion, he functioned throughout his career as an emissary or diplomat.

In February 1822 Fields wrote to Antonio Martínez, then governor of Texas: "What is to be done with us poor Indians? We have some grants that was give to us when we came under the Spanish government and we wish you to send us answer by the next mail whether it might be reversed or not, and if it is permitted we will come as soon as possible to present ourselves before you. . . ."[7] His request opened a lengthy period of negotiations between the Cherokees and the Mexican government.

In November the Cherokee council sent Fields and twenty-two Cherokees southward to San Antonio to meet with the new governor of the Province of Texas, José Felix Trespalacios. The Cherokees convinced Trespalacios that they could be useful to the province, and he recommended them to Colonel Don Gaspar López, commandant general of the Eastern Interior Provinces, the military region of which Texas was a part. Trespalacios explained that the Cherokees wished permission to settle in Texas, and that as governor he had concluded an eight-part agreement with them that he realized must be approved by higher authority in order to be valid.[8]

The articles of this agreement, dated November 8, 1822, permitted Fields and five other Cherokees to travel to Mexico City to seek an audience with Emperor Iturbide. It also allowed Fields to ask the emperor for official approval of his people's present settlement and for permission for Cherokees to continue to emigrate from the United States. Meanwhile, the Cherokees were permitted to remain on their east Texas farms. The seventh article promised "that they shall be considered Hispano Americans, and entitled to all the rights and privileges granted to such." They were also given permission to trade with other inhabitants of the province, both Hispanic and Indian, but they were barred from trading arms and ammunition to the "wandering" tribes.[9]

For their part, Fields and the other delegates agreed to send all but five of their number back to the villages, where they were to begin organizing militia companies to patrol the trails leading across the Sabine into U.S. territory. Trespalacios charged the warriors with stopping the passage of stolen animals into the United States and with punishing any and all "evil-disposed foreigners" who were trafficking in stolen livestock. Finally, one "Kunetand, alias Long Turkey," was to be appointed as premier chief of the Cherokees in Texas and was to be responsible for carrying out the terms of the agreement.[10] "Treaty" in hand, Fields and the delegation struck out for Saltillo. In December he met with Commandant Don Gaspar López, who helped the Cherokees on their way to the Mexican capital with a donation of one hundred pesos.[11]

The Cherokee delegation arrived in the Mexico City at one of the most inauspicious moments in Mexican history. Within the year 1822 a cadre led by Iturbide had taken control of the revolutionary republican government established in 1821. After presiding for a few months with a junta, in May he overthrew it, prorogued the Congress, and established himself as emperor of Mexico. A new junta, established by the emperor in January 1823, promulgated an Imperial Colonization Law, a statute applying primarily to such foreign entrepreneurs as Stephen F. Austin, who had already requested colonization contracts under the republic.[12] The Cherokees, arriving in the city in late January or early February, might have come under the new law, but they never managed an audience with the emperor. Soon Iturbide himself fell victim to a counterrevolution, and on March 19, 1823, he abdicated. Within days a hastily reconstituted congress abrogated all imperial laws and edicts.[13]

Undaunted, Fields immediately petitioned the new congress for assistance, but he received no encouragement. A congressional resolution was passed in April allowing the deputation to return to Texas, supplying them with various necessities, and, while provisionally approving the Trespalacios-Fields agreement of 1822, stipulating that a final decision would be handed down later. On April 27, 1823, this information was transmitted to General Felipe de la Garza, Gaspar López's successor as commandant general of the Eastern Internal Provinces at Saltillo, with the warning that the commandant must try to relocate the Cherokees further into the interior and that he must prohibit further immigration by the tribe's population in the United States. Furthermore, in the future Cherokee diplomats were to be denied passports to travel to the capital. Finally, the missive suggested that a general colonization law would soon come forth from the congress and that a determination could then be made respecting its application to the Cherokees.[14] In June a disappointed Fields led his troupe back to Texas.[15] On the whole, however, the diplomatic mission seemed to have gained some advantage for the Cherokees.

It would have been consistent with Cherokee practice for Fields to report to the council immediately upon his return. He would be able to explain that Mexico, unlike the United States, did not make treaties forcing Indians as cultural entities to occupy designated tracts of land. It also appeared that the Cherokees would probably be received as colonists, should a colonization law be enacted. In the meantime, the Mexican government promised to protect them in their present location. When he presented his report, the diplomat no doubt explained the proposed military alliance, pointing out that cooperating with the Mexican government would earn the Cherokees a measure of protection against advancing American settlement. The council was no doubt quick to realize the advantages of this arrangement.

And over the next eight months Fields and the chiefs evidently put considerable effort into solidifying their situation in east Texas. They faced two serious problems. First, Americans were slowly drifting into the region south and east of the tribe, settling around Nacogdoches and between Nacogdoches and the Sabine, on Attoyac Bayou. This migration began with a trickle and grew to a flood in 1822 and 1823 as news of a Mexican land grant to Stephen F. Austin spread through Louisiana.[16] The Mexican government had not authorized the immigration of these Americans, whom it considered to be undesirable aliens, and it wished to prevent them from settling near and trading with the Indians.[17] The situation became so disturbing to the Cherokees' council that in September 1824 the chiefs complained to the alcalde of Nacogdoches that there were Americans settling illegally on Indian lands.[18]

The Cherokees' second problem was one of defense against the Comanches and Lipan Apaches, who were regularly attacking the northern Mexican frontier, of which the Cherokees were now very much a part. Hunting and trading parties of these tribes frequently came from the south plains to raid enemy villages in central Texas and to meet with friendly tribes to trade horses and slaves for weapons and agricultural produce. The Comanches made war on the Wacos, located on the Brazos River, and also on the Tonkawas, who were located near the Llano and San Saba rivers.[19] Cherokee villages, as well as Hispanic and American settlements, were prime targets for the nomadic tribes.[20] While defending their lives and property, Cherokee warriors died; and by virtue of the rule of vengeance, these deaths must be paid in Comanche and Apache lives.

Soon, the Cherokee chiefs devised a plan for protecting their own settlements while making their services indispensable to the Mexican government. The traditional practice of making alliances was joined with the immediate need for protection against the Comanches. Augmenting the agreement of November 1822, the Cherokees decided to pursue an intertribal alliance of greater magnitude.

In March 1824 Fields, again serving as the Cherokees' diplomatic representative, communicated the council's plans to José Antonio Saucedo, *jefe político* of Texas. Stating that "the Superior government has conceded to me in this province lands sufficient for establishing the part of the tribe of Indians who depend on me . . . ," he went on to add that he had also received a "commission for commanding all the Tribes and Nations of Indians which are in the four Provinces of the East." Accordingly, he said, he had invited the Lipans and Comanches to meet on July 4 at his house on the Sabine River, "in compliance with the order of the Supreme Government," to conclude a treaty of peace. Fields requested that Saucedo send a representative to the council and forward word of Fields's actions to the proper authorities in the capital. Apparently, the chiefs and Fields believed that they could make the Cherokees a pacifying and unifying element among the Texas tribes, thus providing protection for Hispanic settlements and acting as a buffer against Americans across the Sabine.[21] Unfortunately for the Cherokees, several circumstances beyond their immediate control worked against the implementation of the plan.

Prime lands in Texas were soon to be open for colonization. In 1823 and 1824 instruments of government had been written for the Republic of Mexico and for internal divisions of that nation. An *Acta Constitutiva,* adopted on January 31, 1824, and approved as the Federal Constitution in October of that year, established Coahuila and Texas as one state, with Saltillo as its capital. In August the congress passed a Federal Colonization Law delegating to the states the responsibility of promoting internal development through settlement programs. As a general guideline, the federal law allowed each state to admit foreigners as settlers, although preference was to be given to Mexican citizens, among whom no distinction was to be made other than individual merit.[22] In March 1825 the State of Coahuila and Texas promulgated its own colonization law. Under its terms settlers could acquire a league of land (4,428.4 acres) for a nominal fee. Foreigners were eligible, but they must become citizens, convert to Catholicism, and prove good character. Native Mexicans could acquire additional land, up to a maximum of eleven leagues, for an additional fee. Another provision discussed the matter of land for Indians.

According to Article 19, "Indians of all nations bordering on the state, as well as wandering tribes that may be within its limits," were accorded the privileges of trading in local markets and applying for land grants. Stipulations included the regulation that they must "declare themselves in favor of" the nation's religious and legal institutions. They might receive the same quantity of land as the other settlers, but "native Indians" were to receive preference over "foreigners."[23] With this law, a legal mechanism had been provided through which Cherokees, Shawnees, Delawares, and other U.S. tribes might obtain legal title to a permanent home. Presumably, they had only to be aware of the intricacies of the law and to follow the prescribed procedure.

At the moment the state colonization law was made public, several American and European entrepreneurs were in Saltillo patiently awaiting their opportunity. They inundated the government with petitions for colonization schemes. On April 15, 1825, the state granted contracts to three "empresarios," as the new law styled individuals who desired to obtain large blocks of land and introduce companies of settlers into the state. To Haden Edwards, a Virginian residing in Louisiana, went a contract to settle eight hundred families on a tract of land lying west and south of Nacogdoches and including the town itself. Frost Thorn, a New Yorker who had come to Texas as an agent of Barr and Davenport, a Louisiana-based trading house, was permitted to settle four hundred families on a tract north of the Edwards's empresarial grant.[24] The Cherokees' towns lay along the Sabine in the southern part of Thorn's grant and along rivers and creeks in the northern part of Edwards's grant. Forbidden now to travel to the state or national capital, and virtually ignored by Texas officials, the Cherokees were probably unaware of the workings of governments and empresarios. Knowing little or nothing of the new edicts, they only gradually realized that a significant opportunity had been missed.

Meanwhile, during the spring and summer of 1824, Fields and the chiefs went on with the task of uniting Texas tribes in a grand alliance. Cherokee delegations met with bands of Comanches and with other tribes and concluded amicable agreements, but, unable to interest tribal representatives in a July 4 meeting, Fields postponed the general conference until August. When the meeting was finally held on August 20, attendance was poor. On September 1 Fields reported to Jefe Político Saucedo that all except the Comanches and Tonkawas had attended and "accepted the terms offered them," although he neglected to outline the terms to Saucedo. The purpose of the meeting, he said, was "to bring them in union one tribe with another, and all to be under true subordination to our new republican government."[25]

In his role as war chief and diplomat, acting for the Texas

Cherokees as well as for Mexico, Fields failed to secure intertribal agreements for the Cherokee council to ratify. Despite his understanding of both Cherokee culture and Mexican defense needs, and despite his considerable experience in negotiating with a variety of political and cultural groups, he, like so many persons of other cultures, could not understand that the nomadic tribes' fragmentary band-type political organization prevented one band from signing a treaty that would be observed by all bands. The Comanches, Fields explained, were "obstinate" and had recently killed a Cherokee. "For that," he said, "I must have satisfaction. I have done all that I could and have kept the other indians off them so far but if they do not come on better terms than they now are my people will be upon them. I am sorry they broke the treaty so soon that I made with them, and if they do not give satisfaction it will be taken by force and by strength of arms."[26] Despite the existence of an international agreement, the Cherokee law of revenge still took effect, and its operation thwarted the plan.

Lack of success in organizing the indigenous tribes under one banner may have motivated Texas Cherokee leaders to channel their diplomatic efforts toward unifying more tractable and familiar peoples. As early as the spring of 1824 Fields had begun encouraging other homeless Indian peoples to move from the United States to Texas. In April George Gray, a U.S. Indian subagent at Sulphur Fork, Louisiana, reported a rumor that Cherokees in Texas had received a grant of land from the Mexican government, and that he "had lately seen a circular from a half Blood Cherokee, a smart, intelligent fellow who commands those Cherokees, wishing all appressed and dissatisfied Indians to join his Band."[27] It seems clear that Fields and the council were promoting settlement in Texas by U.S. Indians who were being pushed westward. This was a new strategy for achieving stability and for securing a homeland; sheer numbers, some Cherokees reasoned, would weight the balance in their favor.

Several hundred Shawnees and Delawares were ready to move into Mexican territory. Earlier, in 1821 and 1822, the Cherokees in Arkansas had been allied with various villages of Shawnees and Delawares residing on the White River in

Arkansas. All were engaged in almost constant warfare with the Osages. In pursuit of their quarry the united warriors ranged across the Red River, and until late in 1824 there were no Mexican or American military forces to hinder them.[28] At the same time, Cherokees continued to move their villages down to the Red River, and they were followed, or perhaps even accompanied by, villages of Shawnees and Delawares.[29] American military authorities found this situation so bothersome that in late September 1823 Acting Governor Crittenden of Arkansas complained to the U.S. secretary of war that one of the groups that had gone to the Red River had recently come back, and "headed by the most daring and intelligent man in the nation, they continue to roam over the frontier. . . . They have recently made a tour to their Northern brethren on White River and in the name of the Cherokee Nation made an offensive and defensive alliance. . . ."[30] Crittenden and others estimated that eight to ten thousand of the "brethren"—Shawnees, Delawares, Piankeshaws, Potawatamies, Kickapoos, and Senecas—were massed on White River.[31]

In the early 1820s, after the stiffening of Western Cherokee national regulations in Arkansas, several villages of Cherokees moved southward into the valley of the Red River. Leaders of the late arrivals included Blanket, Takatoka, and Tahchee, all of whom had left the Western Cherokees because they disagreed with prohibitions against clan revenge.[32] As early as 1824 Tahchee (also known as Dutch) had declared his intention to move south of the Red River. In the autumn of 1825 he did so, and the Arkansas council disclaimed any responsibility for his present or future actions.[33] From their village on the south bank of the Red River near the mouth of the Kiametia River, Tahchee's warriors continued to harass the Osages, who constantly vied with Cherokees, Delawares, Kickapoos, and Americans settled in the Red River valley. This rivalry concerned both conflict over mutual injuries and a struggle for dominance of hunting and agricultural land in an area that was becoming increasingly crowded. These unsettled conditions prompted the U.S. Army to establish Cantonment Towson near the mouth of the Kiametia in mid-1828.[34] Tahchee and his followers were undeterred by the U.S. military pres-

Tahchee (Dutch), a Cherokee leader who lived in Texas in the 1820s, as portrayed in 1834 by George Catlin. Used by permission of the Thomas Gilcrease Institute of American History and Art, Tulsa, Oklahoma.

ence. They simply moved down to the Sabine River and continued the war. Through the 1820s an ever-increasing number of Cherokees, Delawares, Kickapoos, Shawnees, and others on the Red River and in Texas allied against the Osages, Tawakonis, and others.[35]

Fields's unwarranted assumption of authority over practically all of the tribes in Texas, while acceptable to the Cherokee council, was enough to shock the Mexican government. They would pay attention to the Cherokees at last. In August 1824 Saucedo had sent several of Fields's letters to Minister of Relations Lúcas Alamán, warning that the Cherokees' plan to unite the Texas tribes might "degenerate into an evil of unknown extent" and suggesting that it might be wise for the government to send a military force to protect the frontier.[36] Alarmed, Alamán quickly looked into the situation and replied that documents pertaining to Fields's visit to Mexico in 1822–23 revealed such commission to command the tribes. The minister directed Saucedo to take steps to prevent a pantribal council, using military force, if necessary.[37]

Alamán did not know the conference had already transpired. When he discovered it was past, he wrote to Fields and the chiefs demanding to know whether or not they and the other Indians were plotting with Americans across the border to destroy Hispanic settlements. Fields replied that he had "called a meeting of my people to enable me to answer you," formulating a reply "in open meeting" for the diplomat to deliver. Obviously smarting from the accusation of collusion with Americans, the chiefs reaffirmed their promise to "defend the province in case of trouble, difficulties, contradiction, or fraudulent commerce in violation of her rights." Fields added that the Cherokees "have nothing to do with the Anglo Americans here, and we will not submit to their laws, or dictates, but we do, and always will, submit to the laws and orders emanating from the Mexican nation."[38] Finally, the chief reiterated their offer to keep order among the frontier's Indian residents.

During the late summer and autumn of 1825 the Comanches, Tawakonis, and Lipans aggressively attacked Hispanic and American settlements on the east Texas frontier. Correspondence relating to Indian incursions flew rapidly to and from Nacogdoches, San Felipe (empresario Stephen F. Austin's settlement), and San Antonio. Austin was particularly fearful that the Cherokees were forming an Indian alliance against the settlements. In September he wrote to Jefe Político Saucedo and to Colonel Mateo Ahumada, commandant of Texas, to relay stale news that Fields had declared himself chief of all the tribes and was engaged in such "suspicious" activities as treating with the Comanches, Tonkawas, Wacos, and other tribes. In Austin's judgment, these actions indicated that the Cherokees were discontented because their lands had been granted to Haden Edwards. He further offered the opinion that the Cherokees might be satisfied if the government would immediately grant them land.[39]

Rumors of the Cherokees' intentions rapidly spread, and Austin and other settlers suspected that the autumnal attacks by the Comanches and other tribes were instigated by the Cherokees to blackmail the Mexican government into giving them a land grant.[40] Echoing Austin's sentiments, two citizens who had known Richard Fields previously in his career advised him to abandon this course. John G. Purnell, who lived in Saltillo, contacted the diplomat in October 1825 to warn him that "dreadful may be the consequences" if he continued in such mistaken measures. Purnell said, "If your lands were not granted at a time when the Government was not firmly established, that should not be the cause of war," and he encouraged Fields to "Ask and it will be given you."[41] In November another resident of Saltillo, one "F. Durcy," wrote to Francois Grappe, Fields's father-in-law: "We are surprised to hear about Mr. Fields, the halfbreed; he has placed himself at the head of several savage nations, and has formulated a plan of attacking the new colony of Texas, while because although the government has not given him any land it has not prevented others from establishing themselves." Durcy begged Grappe to try to influence Fields to abandon the plan.[42] All apparently misunderstood the motives of Fields and the Cherokees, and all assumed the worst. It might be appropriate to note that these judgments were based less on fact than on fear and prejudice and, perhaps, on prior experience. Nonetheless, they would continue to worry about the safety of the frontier settlers because they did not perceive the truth about the Cherokees' scheme. At this juncture, an adventurer named John Dunn Hunter came into the Cherokee country. His arrival and, subsequently, his well-intentioned interference in Cherokee politics were to have unfortunate consequences.

John Dunn Hunter came to Texas in 1825. Possessing a remarkable affinity for Indian life, he claimed to have been captured in infancy and raised as a Cherokee. He said that he had been befriended by an Englishman and given a good education; then he had lived with the Osages. It is true that Hunter had traveled widely in the United States and in England, where he had been lionized as a "white savage."[43] Embued with a desire to "save" Native Americans, he wanted to move them out of the path of white settlement by promoting settlement west of the Mississippi River, and he intended to help them become "civilized" and able to live with a world ruled by whites. In 1825, with this goal in mind, he had traveled through Missouri and Arkansas looking for a place to relocate the Quapaws and other tribes. In the autumn of 1825 he had come to Texas in search of a refuge for these peoples.[44]

Hunter was quickly accepted by the Cherokees, who saw in him a ready diplomat who might advance their interests. Attending a council of twenty tribes in November 1825, he appears to have presented himself as a representative of the Quapaws and other tribes residing north and east of the Red River.[45] Fields and Hunter must have instantly agreed on the viability and political expediency of relocating large numbers of U.S. Indians in Mexican Texas. In December 1825 Hunter began a trip to the Mexican capital in search of both a land title for the Cherokees and a tract on which he could settle the Quapaws. The Cherokees financed the excursion, for they had found in Hunter a delegate who could obtain a passport and who, by virtue of his international reputation, might be able to sway the Mexican government in the tribe's favor and bring the Quapaws into Texas as another barrier to American settlement.[46]

Following Hunter's departure, in December Fields, Duwali, and four other headmen visited Nacogdoches, spoke to the alcalde, Samuel Norris, and once again expressed their good intentions. Declaring their friendship for the Mexican government, the chiefs reported that several thousand Shawnees were on their way from the United States with the intention of settling in Texas.[47] Investigating the story, the alcalde learned, no doubt to his surprise, that twelve tribes of U.S. Indians were on the verge of entering Texas.[48] Apparently, the Cherokees' resettlement efforts were about to be successful.

Within the year 1826 there was a considerable immigration to the border region between Texas and the United States. Beginning in January, 170 Shawnees and Delawares settled on Sulphur Fork, in Texas. This movement corresponded to events transpiring east of the Mississippi as Secretary of War John C. Calhoun began in 1825 to implement a plan to clear the Old Northwest of Indians, removing them west of the Mississippi. The Arkansas Cherokee Treaty of 1817, as well as treaties with the Choctaws, Osages, and Kansas had cleared much territory west of the 95th meridian in preparation for receiving Indian immigration from the Old Northwest. Shawnees, Delawares, Kickapoos, Miamis, and other tribes had begun to drift westward across the Mississippi as U.S. agents pressured their leaders for cession treaties.[49]

In April 1825 the Mexican government had granted permission for Shawnees and their allies to settle along the Red River. In 1824 chiefs of the Shawnees, some already residing in the province, had traveled from their villages near Pecan Point and on Sulphur Fork to San Antonio and then to Saltillo to present their request to the governor of Coahuila and Texas. They had asked for a grant of one square mile for each family presently in Texas and for a similar amount for those who would follow. Allied tribes named in the petition included Quapaws, Chickasaws, and Iroquois. Although their petition was tentatively approved by the state's congress, under the colonization law, Coahuila and Texas Governor Rafael Gonzales requested that the national government make a final determination. Accordingly, he forwarded the appropriate documents to Minister of Relations Alamán, and the president approved the settlement under the General Colonization Law of 1824. No mention was made of a land grant, however, and no boundaries were established for the tribe. They were directed to settle along the Red River within twenty leagues of the border (about fifty miles).[50] By mid-1827 there were reportedly more than six hundred families of Shawnees, Kickapoos, and other tribes, in addition to a village of eighty Cherokees, living in the vicinity of Pecan Point on the Red River. According to one observer, the leaders of the Shawnees said that they had come to Texas at the invitation of Richard Fields.[51]

As the immigrant Indian population in northeast Texas increased, Mexican officials in Nacogdoches became increasingly fearful that the tribes might unite for an attack on the frontier settlements. In November 1825 Jefe Político Saucedo and Governor Gonzales persuaded the Mexican secretary of war to send an emissary to the Cherokees. In December Miguel Arciniega, a private citizen of San Antonio, was appointed to this post; his mission was to ferret out the precise nature of the Cherokees' involvement with indigenous and immigrant tribes and "to ascertain whether any such project as that alluded to, exists."[52] Arciniega set out from San Antonio in February 1826; traveling for over a month, he arrived at Nacogdoches in March and was soon making his way toward the Cherokee towns.

Fields met with Arciniega two times, first on the sixteenth of March and again on the nineteenth. It does not appear that they met in a council of the Cherokee elders. Fields managed to convince Arciniega that the Cherokees' intentions were honorable. He also took the opportunity to complain that Americans were making unauthorized settlements on Indian lands.[53] By way of Arciniega, Fields sent a letter to Jefe Político Saucedo, once again explaining the tribe's willingness to police the frontier and to keep the Caddoes, Nacogdoches, Wacos, and other tribes from attacking the peaceful tribes. He also offered the Cherokees' services for a renewed war against the Comanches, should the government be planning one.[54]

Shortly thereafter, Fields received a response to his offer. Saucedo, the political chief, demanded to see copies of any documents the Cherokees might possess verifying their right to occupy their present homes.[55] Although the official offered to send the documentation to "the proper authorities" for approval, he was plainly skeptical of the Cherokees' claim. Although urged to tender the Trespalacios letter and other documents, Fields chose not to do so.

Other Mexican officials did not rebuff the Cherokees so quickly. In April 1826, Mateo Ahumada, the Texas military commandant, planned an attack on the Comanches and other tribes.[56] When he ordered Stephen F. Austin to send local militia against their villages, Austin quickly contacted Richard Fields and asked for the Cherokees' cooperation. He explained that he was giving them a chance to prove "to their new friends the mexicans how useful they can be." The attack was set, he said, for May 25, on the Waco and Tawakoni villages on the Brazos. The Cherokees were asked to attack the Tawakoni village at the headwaters of the Navasota River. Austin assured Fields that "if you turn out in this expedition and destroy the Tawakoni villages . . . it will be the means of securing you land in the country for as many of your nation as wish to remove here. . . . I will promise my aid and friendship in your favor with the Government, and I have no doubt of succeeding. . . ."[57] Counting on the fact that the Cherokees had been recently attacked by Wacos and Tawakonis, Austin reported to Ahumada that he was aligning several tribes to assist the militia.[58] The Cherokees met in council to deliberate on Austin's request.

John Dunn Hunter returned in May, perhaps in time to attend the council and impart the disappointing news that his mission had failed. In return for a grant of land in Texas, he had offered to bring thirty thousand Indians into Mexico to establish communities for border defense. British chargé d'affaires Henry George Ward had promoted Hunter's cause and assisted him in writing a petition to present to President Guadalupe Victoria. Victoria was intrigued by the prospect of having thirty thousand border guards, but U.S. Minister Joel Poinsett, who apparently had the ear of those in power, managed to thwart the plan in order to keep Texas open for purchase by the United States. Hunter presented his petition in March; caught between two nations' maneuverings, it was rejected.[59]

Faced with this political defeat, the Cherokee council decided to accede to Austin's request. The debate must have been spirited, although several of the diplomatic alternatives were hardly palatable. The chiefs might choose to ally with the Wacos and Tawakonis against the Mexicans, but the Cherokees' enmity toward the Comanches, Wacos, Taovayas, and Tawakonis precluded this. The rivalry had already assumed the status of a traditional hostility of the kind previously expressed toward the Osages. Or they might choose neutrality, which could place them in the middle of a battle between Hispanics and colonists on the one hand and the hostile tribes on the other. In any case, they were probably going to be at war with Comanches, Wacos, and Tawakonis in the winter whether or not an alliance was effected with Austin.

Fields and Duwali informed the empresario that the tribe had unanimously agreed to join the alliance, but they had decided to attack the Wacos rather than the Tawakonis. Furthermore, they had decided to delay the attack because the Neches and Trinity rivers were so swollen with flood waters that the spring crops required immediate attention. In the second week in May, however, Ahumada cancelled the planned action, fearing an intertribal war would be carried into the frontier settlements.[60] Now Fields, Duwali, and the chiefs would look for more effective means to secure their newly found homeland. Under intense pressure to take some positive action in their own behalf, Cherokee leaders cast their lot with a group of Americans who promised to help them.

In late 1825 and early 1826 the grant earlier awarded to empresario Haden Edwards was meeting concerted opposition from settlers around Nacogdoches. The land of these original Hispanic occupants of east Texas had been included, perhaps inadvertently, in Edwards's 1825 grant from the State of Coahuila and Texas. Edwards had immediately attempted to collect a fee from original settlers who could not show a legal title to their property. In spring 1826 a political controversy ensued between Edwards and Mexican authorities, particularly Jefe Político José Antonio Saucedo, who took the side of the original occupants of the Nacogdoches area. To make matters worse, Edwards took sides in a battle over the election of a new alcalde for Nacogdoches. He supported his son-in-law, Chichester Chaplain, who was opposed by Samuel Norris, an old settler. Chaplain won the election, but Norris and his followers alleged and proved vote fraud. Saucedo backed Norris, and Chaplain was unceremoniously ousted from his office.[61] Mexican authorities became aware of the unrest between Edwards's colonists and the old settlers, and when the trouble threatened to boil into an armed conflict, the president declared the empresario an outlaw and ordered him arrested. In June the government cancelled Edwards's contract, much to the satisfaction of Saucedo, Norris, and the old settlers.[62] At about the same time, Haden Edwards wisely decided to return to the United States for several months.

Nonetheless, throughout the late summer of 1826, settlers, red and white alike, were in a very troubled and nervous state. In July, Hunter and Fields held a council of leaders of the immigrant tribes to discuss mutual concerns and perhaps to talk over Hunter's plan for mass emigration of Indians from the United States.[63] Shortly thereafter, rumors circulated that Edwards was in league with the Cherokees, that he had "tried to seduce [Fields] into a revolt" when both were in Mexico City, and that the empresario was in Kentucky recruiting seven hundred men to invade and conquer Texas.[64] Other rumors predicted an imminent attack by Comanches; Richard Fields himself fueled this fire with letters to Austin and Norris. The chief warned Austin that the Comanches planned "to attack your colony and destroy it entirely, or compel the settlers to leave it by the beginning of next moon."[65] Fields transmitted a similar note to Alcalde Norris, asking for authority to make war on the Tawakonis, Wacos, Taovayas, and Comanches, who, he said, "have killed some of our people"; the chief ingratiatingly added that "we consider ourselves sons of the Mexicans, and we cheerfully offer our persons and the last drop of our blood for the defense of the country. . . . the son does no wrong when he spills blood in the defense of his down trodden father."[66]

Fields's veiled threat was not lost on the empresario. Austin was convinced, partly because he had heard the same story from other sources. He counseled the authorities to prepare to defend the frontier, and he particulary advised Saucedo to make up for having thus far ignored the Cherokees, noting that "the tardiness in making provisions for the friendly Indians will dissatisfy them; which would be unfortunate, as 100 Cherokee warriors are decidedly superior to 500 Comanches."[67] Saucedo also realized the gravity of the situation, and on September 25 he wrote to Fields, giving him rein to "avenge the offenses" given the Cherokees by the other tribes.[68] The political chief no doubt hoped that this war would keep the Cherokees away from the other settlers and also put them at odds with the very tribes that Fields had earlier attempted to unite.

While Haden Edwards was out of the country, his brother, Benjamin, who had come to Texas during the controversy, took up the task of protecting his brother's interests. He badgered state and local officials to reinstate the colonization contract, and he refused to admit that Edwards no longer had the right to issue land titles. When Haden returned in early October, his followers were in an intensely aggravated state. In November Haden was arrested, under the May decree, by Martin Parmer, one of his own followers who functioned as colonel of militia. Parmer put Edwards on parole, led his militia into town, captured the archives, and court-martialed Alcalde Samuel Norris and other officials. Hearing of this, Saucedo and Colonel Ahumada led a force of militia north to Nacogdoches in December and January. While the governmental army was en route, Parmer, Benjamin Edwards, and their cohorts entered Nacogdoches again and, under a flag carrying the logo "Independence, Liberty, and Justice," seized the Old Stone Fort and proclaimed the Edwards grant to be the Republic of Fredonia.[69]

During the autumn months the Cherokees had been courted by Benjamin Edwards. The empresario's brother had been busy, trying to muster support among the Edwards colonists, but he had only been able to secure the loyalty of thirty men. With uncharacteristic perspicacity he saw an opportunity to involve the Cherokees in the controversy and thereby bolster his forces. The council allowed Fields and Hunter to open negotiations with Edwards, who was able to persuade at least some, if not most, of the Cherokees to support him.[70] On December 21 several Indian leaders went to Nacogdoches, met with leaders of the Fredonian Republic, as Benjamin Edwards had styled it, and signed a treaty of friendship and alliance. Fields's speech during the assembly gave some idea of his people's temperament in these trying times:

> In my old days I travelled 2000 miles to the City of Mexico to beg some lands to settle a poor orphan tribe of Red People that looked up to me for Protection. I was Promisid lands for them after staying one year in Mexico and spending all I had I then came to my People and waited two years and then sent Mr. Hunter again after selling my stock to Provide him money for his expenses when he got there he stated his mission to government they said that they knew nothing of this Richard Fields and treated him with contempt—I am a Red man and a man of honor and cant be imposed on this way we will lift up our tomahauks and fight for land with all those friendly tribes that wishes land also If I am Beaton I then will Resign to fate and if not I will hold lands By the forse of my Red Warriors.[71]

Fields and Hunter then pledged the Cherokees to aid the Fredonians in evicting the unwelcome occupants of the grant. In return, the Cherokees were to receive title to all of Texas lying north of a line drawn from Nacogdoches westward to the Rio Grande. Richard Fields, John Dunn Hunter, Nekolakeh, John Bags, and Cuktokeh signed for the Cherokees.[72]

The Cherokees probably held a large council to consider this important decision. Fields and Hunter, both consummate diplomats, no doubt played up the tribe's recent failures with the Mexican government and by so doing convinced many of the tribe that uniting with the seemingly powerful Fredonians would solve all difficulties. Duwali presumably concurred in the agreement, or at least he could not muster opinion strong enough to change the consensus. Because the pact might involve fighting, the Cherokees' traditional principle of withdrawal from a consensus would operate if the young men were called to arms.

When the alarming news of the Fredonian declaration reached Austin's settlement, the empresario took steps to undo the alliance. Through the joint offices of Peter Ellis Bean, acting as an agent of the Mexican government, and José Antonio Saucedo, most of the Cherokees were dissuaded from adhering to the treaty. Bean wrote to Fields several times telling him that he could expect justice from the Mexican government. Pointing out that the Cherokees had not followed proper procedures for obtaining land, Bean assured Fields that a land grant could be obtained if application were made through the proper channels by agents with acceptable credentials. Fields responded that Bean "was too late; if he had of saw me one month sooner, Perhap[s] we might have come on terms."[73] Saucedo also assured Fields that both the people and the land claim "for your new colony" would be protected, reiterating that the Cherokees needed to send another agent to Mexico.[74] Austin also wrote to Fields, Duwali, and the other chiefs to confirm that the tribe's original land claim would be protected if the Indians dissolved their alliance with the rebels, pointing out that Edwards' contract had been cancelled.[75] Duwali accepted the arguments. In early January Saucedo issued an amnesty proclamation and sent three commissioners to convince the rebels to surrender. Although they did not visit the Cherokees, the commissioners ascertained that Duwali and Gatunwali had refused to join Fields and Hunter in the confederation.[76] Bean also discovered and made use of the division among the Cherokees when he met with Gatunwali, Duwali, several other Cherokees, and chiefs of the Shawnees, Delawares, and Kickapoos on January 25.[77]

While Duwali and other chiefs at first may have been persuaded by Fields's demands for an alliance with the Fredonians, and the customary unanimity may have prevailed in the council in the autumn of 1826, by the first of the new year a factional split had surfaced. With a Mexican army en route to attack the Fredonians, Hunter and Fields's machinations no longer seemed to offer much advantage. Bean's and Austin's arguments and Saucedo's promises had the desired effect, and opponents of the Fredonians held sway in the council. In early February, as Saucedo's army approached Nacogdoches, no Cherokees appeared to reinforce Edwards's minions, and the rebels fled across the Sabine.[78]

Duwali was now left to prove to the victorious Mexican authorities that the Cherokees' momentary intransigence was not to be taken as a disloyal act. Again the elders met in council. What transpired can only be imagined, but it resulted in an order to execute Fields and Hunter. This action was perfectly consistent with tribal law, which held that any individual violating the community interest to benefit an enemy or dealing in tribal lands without permission was to be punished by death.[79] The application of this rule to Fields's situation may well mean that he had refused to repudiate the agreement when the consensus changed. Fields headed for American territory, but he was captured and executed after crossing the Sabine.[80] Hunter escaped but was pursued by a force of Americans, including some of Austin's militia led by Bean. They failed to capture Hunter, but he was later apprehended at the Anadarko village and killed.[81] Duwali and Gatunwali came into Nacogdoches on February 28 to report the execution to the Mexican authorities, bringing with them one of Hunter's guns and a Fredonian flag said to have been hanging in Field's house.[82] Ahumada dutifully reported the same to Anastasio Bustamante, commandant general of the Eastern Interior Provinces, on May 11; in his reply, Bustamante wryly noted that "if there are any public rejoicings, spare the powder and do nothing. . . ."[83] In April the general commended Duwali and Gatunwali ("Bowl" and "Big Mush") to the Supreme Government for their prompt action in the affair.[84]

The Cherokees had spent six years exhausting every opportunity to secure title to their land. While their everyday lives had no doubt gone on as before, devoted to farming, hunting, and making traditional sorties against new and old enemies, their political leaders had followed various avenues of diplomatic interaction with Mexican authorities. That they had not properly followed the procedure required to apply for a land grant under the Colonization Law of Coahuila and Texas was perhaps due to ignorance of the letter of the law, yet authorities in Mexican Texas did not offer much assistance in the application process. Civil chief Duwali and the council sent Hunter to Mexico City to be their advocate, although he, too, was unfamiliar with Mexican law and political manipulation and fell victim to international political maneuvering. After failing in his mission, Hunter persuaded the council to ally with the Edwards brothers and their cohorts in a scheme that was bound to backfire, as Mexican authorities did not brook rebellions of this sort among resident foreigners. The only effect of Cherokees involvement in the Fredonian Rebellion, if it even deserves the appellation, was that Americans in east Texas learned to distrust them. Even Austin did nothing more to help them before he died. Fields's pitiful protests about "poor Indians" notwithstanding, it was evident to Mexican officials, empresarios, and settlers alike that the Cherokees were a diplomatic and military presence henceforth to be both watched and feared.

«»

3

The Calm: Hopeful Accommodation, 1828–1835

"Where stood the Indian of other days? He stood on the shore of the Atlantic, and beheld, each morning, the sun rolling from the bosom of its green waves. In that sun he beheld his *God, and bowed in homage to the shrine. He felt that no intermediate creature could usurp the favor of his Divinity. He was a monarch of the wilds, and his buoyant step proclaimed him 'every inch a King.' That age has long gone by—the aboriginal character is almost lost in the views of the white man, or by a series of impositions. A succession of injuries has broken his proud spirit, and taught him to kiss the hand which inflicts on him stripes. . . ."—Sam Houston, "Tah-Lohn-Tus-Ky," 1830 (in Williams and Barker, eds.,* Writings of Sam Houston *1:156).*

While the leaders of the Texas Cherokees searched for a measure of security in their new homes, their families undoubtedly settled into a daily and yearly routine resembling their previous existence in Arkansas. Although they had changed geographical regions, they brought with them many of their accustomed lifeways, which had been conditioned since 1794 to new and useful material goods. In the seven years between the Fredonian affair and the outbreak of the Texas Revolution, the Cherokees experienced a glimmer of hope for their future in the northern Mexican province.

After attracting attention by cooperating in the abortive 1826 rebellion, the Cherokees came under the scrutiny of the national government. In 1828, General Manuel de Mier y Terán was ordered northward to gather information on the region of northeastern Texas, preparatory to establishing a Mexico–United States boundary; as a corollary, Terán was also directed to investigate rumors that Texas was being overrun by Americans. The Boundary Commission contingent included

French botanist Jean Louis Berlandier, who was to make scientific collections, and Lieutenant José María Sánchez y Tapia, an artillery officer assigned as draftsman.[1] Both were acute observers, and through their accounts posterity was favored with eyewitness (albeit ethnocentric) descriptions of Texas Cherokee life in the late 1820s. Augmenting these official observations are contemporary descriptions provided by the tribe's neighbors.

In 1828 the Cherokees subsisted primarily by farming and raising cattle, according to Sánchez.[2] In practicing riverine agriculture in the old Caddo fields, they probably changed the location of their villages and fields every few years as the soil's fertility declined from overuse. This form of shifting agriculture had long been traditional among the early Cherokees. But after 1794, as conditions of life improved in the East, and heavy implements became available through the U.S. government, the Eastern Cherokees altered their ways. They came to rely upon more intensive agriculture, adopting the cultivation of cotton and grains, which required many tools and numerous laborers and tended to make settlements more permanent.[3] Competiton for an increasingly limited game supply also made farming and herding more attractive. When Cherokees had moved westward across the Mississippi, thereby removing themselves from ready sources of manufactured goods, they had fortunately been able to rely on hunting and trapping and on traditional agricultural practices. In addition, they returned to traditional seasonal pursuits: spring was for planting; summer was for tending crops; autumn was harvest time; and winter was the primary season for hunting, trapping, moving village sites, and making war. Gradually, as manufactured goods became more available through trade, and as wealthier emigrants brought with them herds of cattle and horses, life in the West grew more comfortable and more similar to life in the East. In 1811, the year of Duwali's first emigration, headman Kiamee reported from Missouri that Western Cherokees "have good corn fields. We have plenty of cattle and hogs. We have plenty of Buffaloe and Deer," and that the women made cotton cloth.[4] For instance, Duwali's entourage had included a large herd of cattle and horses. Cherokees coming into Texas acquired the necessities of life by hunting, gathering, farming, and trading. By 1833 a population of 800 Texas Cherokees supported themselves by agriculture and reportedly owned 3,000 cattle, 3,000 hogs, and at least 500 horses.[5] They grew corn, peas, squash, other vegetable crops, and cotton, but apparently they did not have the resources required to grow small grains.[6]

Migration itself worked to promote instability, as villagers in transit needed to stop every spring to plant. They would stay long enough to harvest the crops in the fall and would move on in the winter, which was usually the hunting season. In this way, Duwali's village had come to Texas. Yet even after their arrival in Texas, his people continued to shift their village locations whenever necessary. In 1828, Duwali's village was on the Sabine; by 1835 it was on Cherokee Creek, nine miles north of present-day Henderson. By 1836 he had moved it to a location on Bowles Creek, between present Henderson and Tyler. Two years later it lay near the Neches Saline, four miles west of present-day Alto.[7] Similarly, Gatunwali's village was once located in present northwestern Rusk County and later was moved to a spot a few miles south of the present community of Rusk.[8] Richard Fields's village, which in 1823 lay on the Sabine, had been moved by 1825 to Cypress Creek, a tributary of the Sulphur Fork in present-day Cass County.[9]

In 1828 there were between eighty and one hundred Texas Cherokee families, and the total population probably numbered between three and four hundred.[10] As far as can be determined from contemporary descriptions, there were at least three and perhaps as many as seven towns.[11] Most of the villages lay north of Nacogdoches along the Sabine River and its tributaries, including a stream now known as Cherokee Creek. In 1828 this region lay within the land granted to empresario Frost Thorn.[12] In 1825 one village of Cherokees existed on the Red River near the mouth of the Kiametia River. Its leader, Tahchee, alternately moved the village back and forth north and south of the Red River as circumstances dictated.[13] After 1829, when the Western Cherokees signed a treaty exchanging their Arkansas lands for new homes in present-day Oklahoma, the Texas Cherokee population expanded.[14] In 1833

Duwali estimated their numbers at eight hundred persons, most residing within the Department of Nacogdoches, along the Sabine.[15]

While agriculture was their primary pursuit, hunting and gathering probably remained as important sources of subsistence for the Texas Cherokees as they were for other frontier folk. Traditionally, gathering fruits, nuts, and berries was the spare-time occupation of women, children, and old folks; men were the hunters and would pursue a variety of game including deer, bison, bear, beaver, otter, raccoons, rabbits, snakes, turkeys, turtles, and fish. In winter they brought in fresh meat, and from their catch they were able to "harvest" many skins for trade.[16] In 1819 Thomas Nuttall, on his tour through Arkansas, had remarked that some of the Cherokees maintained hunts similar to those held by Plains tribes. As late as the 1830s the Arkansas Cherokees were still participating in lengthy winter hunts.[17] Duwali and his followers continued the practice, for it was a means to underwrite normal subsistence as well as obtain various animal skins, which were all valuable trade commodities in the local market.[18]

Texas Cherokee women spent some of their time producing textiles, woven from cotton grown in their own fields. Cherokees had been growing cotton since the late eighteenth century, weaving it on a loom of their own invention until 1794, when the U.S. agency had begun providing them with cotton cards and spinning wheels.[19] According to Antonio Bulfe, who acted as interpreter for the Mexican government, in 1824 the Texas Cherokees were weaving cotton cloth and making garments.[20] Cotton was another commodity they could use to barter for manufactured goods still scarce in Texas.

The Texas Cherokees participated in east Texas's regional market system by trading with American and Hispanic settlers. Sánchez mentioned in 1828 that the Cherokees were pursuing a lively trade, bringing skins, vegetables, livestock, and cotton cloth to the Nacogdoches marketplace.[21] In the same year, empresario Frost Thorn, who lived near the town, wrote that he had bought more than one thousand dollars' worth of "corn and pease" from the Cherokees for his colonists.[22] In the late 1830s Duwali was augmenting his subsistence activities by working a salt mine at the Neches Saline and bartering the product for various goods.[23] By trade, the Cherokees obtained hardware, metal, cloth, firearms, and ammunition, as well as such implements as plows, spades, and hoes to help maintain shifting agriculture.[24]

Just as in the case of their subsistence economy, house building seems to have changed little as the Cherokees adapted to their Texas environment. In the eighteenth century both Lieutenant Henry Timberlake and William Bartram had described Cherokee dwellings as square houses, usually constructed of logs, containing two or three rooms and measuring almost sixteen feet wide and sixty feet long.[25] Beside the dwelling a small sweathouse was built. Nuttall commented on Western Cherokees' dwellings in similar terms. In addition, he noted that houses were finished with wattle and daub plaster and were roofed with bark.[26] Texas Cherokee homes were described in similar terms by Jean Louis Berlandier and Sánchez in 1830.[27] In Texas, as among the Arkansas branch of the Western Cherokees, dwellings were grouped into communities.[28]

Towns played an important role in Texas Cherokee life. These centers may have served ceremonial, and perhaps even redistributive, purposes. While aboriginal Cherokee towns were clusters of dwellings sometimes fortified by an exterior palisade, by the eighteenth century the typical community was a village comprising thirty to forty households, generally dispersed over a large area, with dwellings in proximity to various cultivated fields.[29] In 1828 Frost Thorn described one community lying on his grant as "a compact settlement."[30] In early times crops had been harvested communally and stored in granaries in the town, and at various times the "uku" and council had distributed the grain to kin groups. This practice declined, and a more individualistic style of farming developed after 1794. However, the town did continue to function as a ceremonial and political center. Councils still met in a central town-house. In 1828 Cherokees living in Duwali's village on the Sabine River received Sánchez and other representatives of Terán's expedition in a brush structure twenty-five yards long by ten yards wide. Assuming that this building served at least a few of the same communal purposes in the nineteenth century as had the town-houses of the previous century, it would have been used primarily for intertown and intertribal councils and as a community center for ceremonial observances.[31]

Ceremonies had always been an important part of life for the Cherokees because ritual functioned to keep human beings and nature in harmony and to maintain the world in balance. In ancient times life had been circumscribed by a great ceremonial cycle. The Cherokee year was divided into the cold months, extending from early October through April, and the warm months, extending from May through September.[32] The cold season was the time of major ceremonies and hunting. In a "first new moon of autumn" ceremony the people marked the beginning of the winter months and celebrated the creation of the world with ritualized hunting and bathing and with fasting.[33] Ten days later came a feast of reconciliation, with fasting, hunting, cleaning of the council house, and lighting of a new sacred fire. Symbolizing purification and renewal, this was the most important festival in the annual cycle.[34] Other ceremonies were held later to ward off death and disease and to celebrate the waning of winter.[35] In May came the warm season, a time for war and for cultivation. At the direction of the council, men and women cooperatively cleared fields and planted seeds. The men played ball games and made sorties against their enemies while the women gathered fruit and tended fields.

The only rite actually observed to be practiced in Texas was the green corn ceremony. In early autumn, before the cooperative harvest, a preliminary green corn ceremony and a final green corn ceremony celebrated the ripening of crops. Traditional proceedings involved fasting, dancing, ritualized hunting, and veneration of the peace chief.[36] The Cherokees and other immigrant tribes in Texas conducted the first-fruits ceremony in August, near the end of the warm season; observers at these ceremonies in 1828 and in 1835 noted that these were scenes of great revelry.[37] Other ceremonies may well have been conducted privately, or without being recognized by other settlers or by Mexican authorities.[38]

Other more obvious aspects of Cherokee life were immediately noticed by investigators in 1828. Sánchez was particularly impressed by the Indians' style of clothing, which reflected the acculturative tendencies of their Arkansas kinsmen at the time of separation. Describing their "cotton dresses," he lamented their lack of ornamentation.[39] Jean Louis Berlandier, the French naturalist, used Sánchez's detailed descriptions to flesh out a verbal portrait: the dress of Cherokee women, he said, "resembles that of French peasant girls." Some of them, he said, "have begun to acquire a bit of European taste in their toilettes."[40] Cherokee women possessed looms and wove "parti-colored textiles" with which they fashioned their family's clothing.[41]

A contemporary watercolor illustration done from information and sketches provided by Sánchez gave visual evidence of Cherokee dress. In it, the Cherokee woman wears an "empire" style dress (one typically worn by European and American women of the era) with long tapered sleeves, long skirt, and high waist. Her hair is braided and wound around the crown, and on her feet are European-style slippers. The man wears a red turban, a cloth tunic or coat bound at the waist by a red sash, skin leggings with cloth garters below the knee, and moccasins. In his belt is a pipe tomahawk, a typical part of Cherokee male attire at this time.[42] These descriptions generally correspond to Nuttall's observations on Cherokee attire in Arkansas. Although the naturalist did not mention turbans, such were typical of nineteenth-century southeastern Indian headgear in general. In a well-known 1828 portrait, Sequoyah wore a turban, and in George Catlin's 1830s portraits of Tahchee and John Jolly, these chiefs wore turbans.[43]

The Cherokees' interest in education also intrigued the authorities. In Arkansas the education of youth had become popular, and the Texas Cherokees mirrored the practice. They maintained a school for their children, and many of the tribe could read and write.[44] Berlandier noted, "Those who live in Texas keep in constant touch with their compatriots of the northern states [Arkansas], writing to each other in their own alphabet. . . ."[45] He no doubt referred to the Cherokee syllabary, which had been compiled by Sequoyah in 1821 and

"Cheraquis" of Texas in 1828, as depicted in a watercolor executed by Lino Sánchez y Tapia, from descriptions given by José María Sánchez y Tapia, of the 1828 Terán expedition. Used by permission of the Thomas Gilcrease Institute of American History and Art, Tulsa, Oklahoma.

brought by Sequoyah himself into the Arkansas region in 1822.[46] Cherokees of all walks of life on both sides of the Mississippi River readily adopted this form of writing. That some Texas Cherokees were literate in their own language is also evidenced by letters written in the Cherokee syllabary during the early 1830s.[47]

The political structure of the Texas Cherokees seems to

have paralleled that of the Western Cherokees in general. Although there is no specific description of the dual nature of village government per se, it may be inferred from contemporary accounts that each village was a chiefdom in the traditional fashion. There is also evidence that individual towns sent representatives to regional council meetings to determine diplomatic policy for the corporate group. Berlandier pointed out that "total authority is never invested in a single individual. In a plenary assembly they appoint two chiefs, one to command the armed forces, the other to serve as political ruler of the tribes."[48] In this regional dual organization, which mirrored the system of the Western Cherokees in Arkansas, tribal leaders Richard Fields, John Bags, Nekolakeh, and others served as diplomats and war chiefs in the early 1820s. They were sent on missions to negotiate with friendly tribes and with the Mexican government as well as on forays against enemy Indian nations. After Fields's execution in 1827, Gatunwali ("Hard Mush") assumed the post of war chief and diplomat. Duwali functioned as the primary civil chief during the Cherokees' entire period of residence in Texas.[49]

When Gatunwali hosted Sánchez and the others of the Terán delegation in 1828, posterity was afforded a rare glimpse of the traditional procedure followed in intervillage council meetings. Sánchez observed that the Cherokees were governed by two chiefs, "Wols" (Duwali) and "Mush" (Gatunwali). The two received Terán's expedition in the town-house of Duwali's village during an intertribal council. The leaders of several other immigrant nations in Texas, including the Shawnees and perhaps others, were arranged in a circle on the floor. "In the middle of the circle," said Sánchez, "they spread a buffalo skin upon which the political chief, Musch [*sic*] placed twenty-one strings of white beads which he took out of a little case, while others held a white flag fixed on a pole." This type of protocol, utilizing beads of a properly symbolic color, was customary, and in this case the white beads symbolized peace.[50] In his speech to the assemblage Gatunwali noted that the beads were tokens of friendship offered according to ancient custom. This chief's function as diplomatic leader is apparent. Sanchez's description of "Musch" as

#368

To the Committy of Safety of Nacodoches or whom it may concern

I am instructed by the Chief of the Cherokee tribe through his interpreter to inform you that they have been Misrepresented by some Mischief Making person a great deal to his displeasure. The person so offending is a Mr H. M. Willson who has been staying among the tribe some days but has left for Nacogdoches thence to the United States and it is requested that he be apprehended and chastised according to what he deserves

The Chief expresses that he is very sorry that they have been so misrepresented as it has caused all the families that the report has reached to leave their homes taking what they could pack off and leaving their stock &c exposed. The offender has reported that when he left the indians were assembled in hostile array, and that he escaped with some difficulty, and that he had no doubt but that several white persons of his acquaintance with myself were killed, which is not the case, but that every thing is as it was, all in peace and quietude, and that it is his, the Chiefs particular request so to remain. The Chief also say that the persons reported to

April 13 1836

Manuscript letter written by "Big Mush, chief of the Cherokee tribe," to the Nacogdoches Committee of Safety, on April 13, 1836; the letter contains

have been killed are at this time present and
that he looks upon them with friendship and
to satisfy you that they, the indians, are as
they were before, in peace, he sends you the
compromise, or understanding which was under-
stood when they were misrepresented last fall
or winter

Big Mush
Chief of the Cherokee tribe

April 13th 1836
at head quarters

By [illegible]

sixteen lines written in the Cherokee syllabary. Used by permission of the Texas State Library, Austin, Texas.

"political chief" reveals his lack of familiarity with Cherokee diplomatic methods: as war chief in charge of diplomacy, Gatunwali would have been responsible for meeting with deputations of foreigners. Another war chief, Nekolakeh, also known as Black Leg or John Negro Legs, spoke in the meeting, as did the Shawnee delegate. Duwali, as civil chief, remained quietly in the background. The purpose of the conference, reaffirmation of an intertribal alliance against the Tawakonis and Wacos, was accomplished.[51]

As is obvious from this council, war prompted by clan revenge remained an ongoing activity for Cherokees in Texas. Its perpetuation testifies to the persistence of traditional kinship reckoning and clan obligations among the Texas Cherokees. Cherokees living in Texas still clashed with the Osages as well as with new enemies—the Wacos, Tonkawas, Tawakonis, and Comanches of Texas. In Arkansas, despite efforts of John Jolly and other chiefs to restrict the operation of clan revenge by enacting prohibitory legislation, and despite the efforts of American officials to end intertribal rivalry for hunting territory by arranging peace treaties, the Cherokee-Osage conflict continued, frequently spilling over into Texas.[52]

During the mid-1820s Cherokees and Osages were often locked in combat along the tributaries of the Red River. Here frontier conditions were so unsettled that the U.S. Army sent a reconnaissance party into Mexican Texas to investigate the immigrant tribes residing there. In August 1827 Lieutenant William S. Colquhoun traveled from Fort Towson south of the Red River to a Shawnee village, where he attended a council being held by the Shawnees, Delawares, and Kickapoos. He requested that they agree to a hold a peace conference with the Osages, but they refused. Colquhoun estimated that the combined fighting strength of the Shawnees, Delawares, Kickapoos, Cherokees, Creeks, and Choctaws in the vicinity was 500 warriors.[53] While war with the Osages continued to occupy the Cherokees on Red River until the relocation of the Osages on a reservation in Kansas after 1825, the Cherokees living along the Sabine were drawn into war with the Wacos, Tawakonis, and Comanches in the late 1820s.

In 1827 hostilities between Texas tribes erupted anew. As

the population of immigrant Indians and Americans increased in east Texas in the first three decades of the nineteenth century, game became correspondingly scarce. Each year, after their spring plantings and fall harvests, Cherokees, Shawnees, Delawares, and other immigrant tribes ventured further and further afield in search of deer and buffalo. Over and over again they tangled with nations to the west. Clashes resulted in injuries, death of a kinsman demanded revenge, and the cycle of vengeance was renewed. Occasionally, Cherokees from the north traveled across the Red River to aid their clan brothers. In 1827, for instance, a party of Arkansas Cherokees led by John Smith came to Texas to avenge the death of clan brothers slain earlier in the year. After holding a three-day council at Gatunwali's village, Duwali, Gatunwali, and Tahchee, presumably all of the same clan, joined their followers with Smith's for an assault on a Tawakoni village on the Brazos River.[54]

Meanwhile, as the Cherokees and other immigrant tribes went about their normal everyday pursuits, circumstances in Mexico worked in their favor. General Manuel de Mier y Terán, whom they had hosted in their villages during his 1828 tour, had since become commandant general of the Eastern Interior Provinces. His inspection of Texas had left him concerned about Americans who were slipping across the Mexico–United States border with, as he noted, "their constitution in their pockets," and taking up residence on property belonging to the original settlers around Nacogdoches as well as on land granted to promoters of colonization. Terán's formal recommendations to the Mexican government were threefold: garrison Texas with enough troops to defend the border; encourage and regulate coastal trade between Texas and Mexico; and colonize the region with Mexicans and Europeans. A corollary to this last aim was to utilize the Cherokees and other nonindigenous Indian settlers as a buffer.[55]

Terán's recommendations were adopted by the Mexican government and were made effective with the Law of April 6, 1830. This statute, which was considerably harsher than Terán had anticipated, cancelled all current empresario contracts, with the exception of those under which colonies had already been established; outlawed further immigration from the United States; created an office of commissioner of colonization to oversee the settlement of Texas; and provided for garrisons to be stationed within Texas.[56] Terán was chosen to serve as colonization commissioner.

The commissioner's plan could have greatly benefited the Cherokees and other immigrant Indian nations, but the reality of land ownership in east Texas was already complicated. The Cherokees' villages lay in the center of a region already granted to an empresario, Frost Thorn. In 1825 he had received a colonization contract to settle four hundred families in a colony lying between Haden Edwards's grant and the U.S. boundary,[57] but, as he pointed out in 1828, his land was "totally occupied by Indians," notably Cherokees and Shawnees living along the Sabine and Trinity.[58] When Thorn failed to introduce the requisite number of colonists, his grant was nullified. In 1831 the Mexican government gave the southern portion of his grant, where the Cherokees lived, to General Vicente Filisola, an Italian officer in the Mexican army. In his contract, Filisola agreed to settle six hundred families. Haden Edwards's grant, upon which many Shawnees and Kickapoos resided, was not cancelled until 1827; nontheless, in 1826 the same region was awarded to David G. Burnet, a New Jerseyan who had practiced law in Ohio before taking up residence in Mexico.[59] Burnet's contract lapsed with the Law of April 6, 1830. Fortunately for the Cherokees, neither Burnet nor Filisola had managed to recruit many colonists.

In the summer of 1831 Terán set in motion a procedure to make the Cherokees property owners. On August 15 he ordered José María Letona, governor of the Mexican State of Coahuila and Texas, to send the following directive to Ramon Musquiz, jefe político of the Department of Bexar:

> To comply with the promises made to the Cherokee tribe of Indians, by the Supreme Government, and consulting the preservation of peace with the agricultural Tribes, I have proposed them their settlement on a fixed tract of land, and they having selected it on the Headwaters of the River Trinity and the Banks of the Sabine, I request Your Excellency, to cause that

> they be put into the possession of the same with the corresponding titles.[60]

Colonel José de las Piedras, commandant of Nacogdoches, was directed to carry out the order by helping the Cherokees retain an attorney to assist with the paperwork.[61]

Putting the Cherokees in possession of the land proved to be more difficult than Terán had anticipated, however. Musquiz informed Letona he was prepared to follow orders, but that it would be "difficult to procure and pay the expenses of an attorney" because the Cherokees were so poor.[62] For some reason, Musquiz dragged his feet; he argued that the Cherokees would be embarrassed because they would not be able to pay the commissioner and surveyor, pay for the stamp paper, or pay the land fee required under the present law. He suggested that they be taken in as colonists under an empresario instead. Terán won out, however, and the stamp paper was furnished to Piedras for the Cherokees.[63] Presumably, Piedras contacted Duwali, who must have called a council to review the long-awaited Mexican offer.

Musquiz was accurate in his estimate of the Cherokees' inability to follow through with an application, whether for title as a nation or as individuals under an empresario, but he was right for all of the wrong reasons. Their goal now within their grasp, the Cherokees hesitated. There were important reasons why the Cherokees could not take advantage of this opportunity. Certainly, they had no money; despite their participation in the regional market system, their subsistence economy remained basically nonmonetary. But a more convincing explanation lies in their history and in Cherokee cultural values. For almost two centuries of diplomatic maneuverings with European nations and with Americans, they had become accustomed to conducting treaty negotiations for land cessions. They were not prepared to follow a procedure such as that recommended by Piedras for filing for land. Furthermore, in 1827 they had eliminated Richard Fields, the one man of practical experience who might have assisted them in moving the paperwork through the Mexican bureaucracy. None of the other Cherokees had acquired experience in following legal procedures to acquire land titles. Later events might have had less impact had the Cherokees obtained a Spanish document giving title to their land, but, not being prescient, they were unable to predict what the future would hold.

Terán's vague reference to "corresponding titles" may have constituted another subtle obstacle. If he meant to give the Cherokees individual titles to separate parcels of land, or if they interpreted his meaning so, their council surely might have rejected the offer, as landholding was generally a communal, rather than an individual, concept among the Cherokees. Tradition recognized three types of property ownership: tribal, lineage, and individual. Some real property, such as hunting territory, was owned communally; lineages had rights to work particular fields, keep the harvest therefrom, and hold houses and outbuildings; individuals owned chattel, including household goods, tools, clothing, weapons, animals, and slaves (although there is no evidence of slaveholding by Texas Cherokees).[64] For cultural reasons, then, holding land in severalty might not have been acceptable to these Indians.

Unfortunately, after this initial flurry of activity in 1832, the Cherokees saw their dealings eclipsed by an uprising of colonists against Mexican officials who were enforcing the Law of April 6, 1830, at Anahuac and Velasco. In May and June Commandant Piedras was absent from Nacogdoches while investigating the incidents. Scarcely a month later, he was enmeshed in a dispute in Nacogdoches between Centralists, on the side of the incumbent national government of Mexico, and Federalists, both Hispanic and American, who were rallying around López de Santa Ana in an attempt to overthrow the Centralist govermment.[65]

Watching their opportunity evaporate before their very eyes, the Cherokees sent a party to the commandant's assistance. Duwali, despite his great age, led sixty of his men to Nacogdoches, but they failed to reach Piedras before he surrendered. On August 5, 1832, Piedras abandoned the town to the Federalists.[66] Shortly thereafter, Frost Thorn wrote to Stephen F. Austin that "it required much explanation to counteract his [Piedras's] influence over the Cherokees."[67] In the future, the Cherokees' apparent willingness to help Mexican against Texan would incense the Americans living around Nacogdoches.

Subsequent political events further lessened the possibility that the Cherokees would ever see a positive result from General Terán's plan. By the end of 1832 Federalists under Santa Ana had ousted the Centralist government. In 1832 the general committed suicide, and General Vicente Filisola, upon whose grant the Texas Cherokees lived, was appointed to serve as commandant general. In the same year Governor Letona died of yellow fever. With Piedras, Letona, and Terán gone, the paperwork was never to be completed.[68]

In October 1832 Texans opposed to the Law of April 6, 1830, convened at San Felipe. Fifty-one delegates from sixteen Texas municipalities framed various resolutions respecting the status of Texas under Mexican law, but, for the Cherokees, this body's most important resolution expressed friendship for the immigrant Indians and supported their land claim.[69] Plainly, this effort was made more for purposes of mollification than anything else, but the Cherokees were perhaps unaware of the political machinations in San Felipe or in Mexico. They were, however, aware that they had been about to receive a duly authorized and completely legal title to their settlements and that the momentum would be lost if they now hesitated.

In 1833 Duwali himself took charge of the negotiations with the Mexicans. This marked a significant change in the way in which the Texas Cherokees conducted foreign affairs. Under normal circumstances the most prominent war leader handled negotiations, but in this stressful time the ever-adaptable Cherokees chose their most able and respected advocate to lead the desperate mission. In July 1833, despite his more than seventy years, Duwali traveled to San Antonio, taking with him several of his councillors, to discuss the matter of the unfinished paperwork.

In the middle of the warm season, with crops in the ground, Duwali and five of his councillors met with Miguel Arciniega, the interim political chief of the Department of Bexar.[70] The chiefs presented a petition asking the Mexicans to follow through and grant the tract of land specified in 1831. The boundary, they said, began the crossing of the Bexar Road over the Trinity River, ran eastward along the road to the Angelina River, up the east bank of the Angelina to the house of José Durst and north to the Sabine, westward up the north bank of the Sabine to its headwaters, due west to the Trinity River, and down the west bank of the Trinity to the Bexar (San Antonio) Road crossing.[71] This included the headwaters and valleys of the three major rivers in east Texas, the Trinity, Neches, and Sabine. It also included settlements of Cherokees, Shawnees, Kickapoos, Kichais, and perhaps Delawares and Taovayas, although the Cherokee leaders did not claim land for any of these tribes.[72] Duwali protested that numerous Americans, claiming land titles, had moved into the territory in question. He requested their immediate removal, alleging that most of them had come into the region after General Terán had set the land aside for the Cherokees. The petition was presented by "Colonel Boles, John Boles, Richard Jestice, Piggion, Andrew M. Vann, and Eli Harlin [*sic*]."[73]

Soon after, in August, Duwali, Vann, and Harlan journeyed into Mexico, under a permit from Arciniega. After conferring with Governor Veramendi in Monclova, the capital of Coahuila and Texas, they returned in early September with a letter from the governor. Dated August 21, 1833, this epistle stated that the Cherokees must not be disturbed until the national government had reviewed their case.[74] Hearing of this from Peter Ellis Bean, the Indian agent for Mexico, the political chief hastened to secure a copy of the governor's letter. He questioned the alcalde of Nacogdoches about it, and over the next few months officials argued back and forth over the probable existence of such a document.[75] Finally, in February 1834 the Cherokees proffered their copy. It was indeed from the governor, who noted that the Cherokees were residing on Burnet's and Filisola's grants and that no determination could be made until these empresarial contracts expired.[76] For all of his effort, Duwali and his people were no better off than before.

Meanwhile, the Cherokees and other immigrant nations found themselves in an increasingly tenuous position. They were constantly crowded by an expanding American population in east Texas. Settlers were filling the empty space between Ayish Bayou, on the east of Nacogdoches, and the Trinity River, on the west. Lying in the southernmost portion of the Cherokees' claim, in 1829 this area had reported only 164 households, or 759 persons, and the number had remained constant through 1832. After that, the population increased rapidly. By 1835 the number had jumped to 252 households, or a population of somewhere between 1,100 and 1,500; Tenehaw and Sabine, directly east of the Cherokees' settlements, reported 479 households, or approximately 1,500 persons.[77] West of the Cherokees, in present Anderson County, settlement had begun in 1833 and communities were established at Parker's Fort and Brown's Fort. The influx between 1830 and 1834 was due to illegal immigration, as well as to the lifting of immigration restrictions by Santa Ana in May 1834 and to the efforts of the Galveston Bay and Texas Land Company's commissioner, who began issuing titles in that year.[78]

In 1834 Commissioner of Colonization Juan Almonte, visiting the region, estimated the Indian population of the Department of Nacogdoches (created in 1834 and including most of the territory east of the Trinity) to be approximately 4,500, including 500 Cherokees, 500 Choctaws, 600 Creeks, 400 Shawnees, and 800 Kickapoos, as well as 100 Tejas, 300 Nacogdoches, 500 Coushattas, and 500 Caddoes. The non-Indian population of the entire Department of Nacogdoches he calculated to be 9,000, probably a slight overestimate. Most of the Department's population resided south of the Cherokees.[79] Bordered on the west and south by colonists, with illegal immigrants an unnumbered threat on the north and east, the Cherokees were to know only one more year of relatively peaceful existence.

Mexico, including Texas, was in political disarray in 1834 and 1835. Santa Ana became president of Mexico in 1833 and gradually undermined the Constitution of 1824 with a series of reactionary decrees, eventually abrogating the Constitution in 1834. In reaction against Santa Ana's policies, citizens created disturbances in the states of California, Zacatecas, and Coahuila and Texas; in May 1835 the general led an army to Zacatecas and crushed the insurgents. Texans, too, remained defiant. Committees of Safety were organized in numerous towns, and many protests were voiced by those who favored armed resistance and even separation from Mexico. In July General Martín Perfecto de Cós, Santa Ana's brother-in-law and commandant of the Eastern Interior Provinces from the summer of 1834, arrested several of the resistance leaders. Two months later Cós marched an army from Monclova into Texas, and in mid-October his troops occupied San Antonio. In August Texans (representing both the American and Hispanic population) called for a convention to meet at San Felipe in October. After meeting briefly in Washington-on-the-Brazos, the delegates reconvened in San Felipe and set up a provisional government for Texas. In November the Consultation, as it was called, declared in favor of the Constitution of 1824, elected Henry Smith of Nacogdoches as governor, selected a slate of officers to assist him, and appointed Sam Houston to command all troops other than those besieging San Antonio. In October Santa Ana replaced the Constitution with the *Siete Leyes*, which centralized the government and replaced the states with departments whose governors were appointed and controlled by the dictator. Nevertheless, Texans continued to fight; that December they recaptured San Antonio, and General Cós fled.[80]

Around Nacogdoches and northward into the Cherokee settlements, all was fairly quiet in 1835 as revolutionary events transpired elsewhere. The Cherokees seemed unaware of the controversy. Duwali continued to appeal to the alcalde of Nacogdoches for a resolution of the land question; but he was met with the disappointing news that Burnet's contract had been renewed and extended through December 1835.[81] In February of that year Duwali and his chiefs held a council to debate the alternatives. They might unite all of the tribes in their region and use the alliance to coerce the government into giving them their present settlements; or they might continue to wait for the government to decide on a course of action, meanwhile hoping for Burnet's colonization scheme to collapse.[82]

Whichever course they decided to follow, the Cherokees were in a good position to negotiate. In March Colonel Domingo Ugartechea, military commandant at Bexar, sent Peter

Ellis Bean as emissary to ask the Cherokees and their neighbors to make war on the Comanches. This would stir up the frontier and distract the revolutionaries with defense problems. After a council, the Cherokees promised 500 warriors.[83] But in August, when Jim Bowie visited the Shawnees and Cherokees in anticipation of the campaign against their mutual enemies, both were holding green corn dances and refused to go.[84] In this instance the ceremonial aspect of life took precedence over diplomatic activities. More practical reasons may also have conditioned the Cherokees' refusal to participate in the attack; it was in their interest to continue playing the Texans against the Mexicans in the hope that Mexico might offer them a land grant.

In May the Congress of Coahuila and Texas passed a resolution authorizing the governor to select vacant lands within the state, move the "tribes of friendly and civilized Indians who have emigrated to Texas" into the reservation, and use them as a line of defense against the Comanches.[85] Apparently, no one in an official capacity in Saltillo (now the capitol of the state) or in the Department of Nacogdoches took much notice of the new law, fortunately for the Cherokees and other immigrant tribes. In any case, it is doubtful that any of the tribes would have agreed to abandon their settlements and move onto the frontier. With a revolution brewing in Texas, the Mexican government may have found it prudent to cultivate the friendship of the tribes and leave them in east Texas as a threat to any settlers who might entertain notions of rising against the government.

News that the Cherokees might be aligning with the Mexicans, even for the purpose of chastising the Comanches, alarmed many Texans. In September Duwali and Gatunwali held another intervillage council and sent assurances to Houston and the Texans that they were interested in remaining at peace. Houston invited them to a council on the Brazos and encouraged them to bring the Shawnees and others.[86]

The Cherokees found in Sam Houston a sympathetic and eloquent advocate. Houston's romantic and dynamic story is well known.[87] He had been adopted by Chief John Jolly perhaps as early as 1809 or 1810 when the young adventurer had run away to live with the Cherokees along the Hiwassee River in Tennessee, where Jolly, Duwali, and Talontuskee lived. This form of adoption was common among the Cherokees, and, as an adoptee, Houston would be able to participate in clan activities, assume kinship obligations, and take a Cherokee marriage partner. In 1829 he had moved to Arkansas, joining his adoptive father, John Jolly, who had become principal chief of the Western Cherokees. In Arkansas Houston had made his living as a lawyer, merchant, and citizen of the Western Cherokee Nation. Furthermore, he had married a Cherokee woman, Talihina (also known as Diana) Rogers, daughter of John Jolly's brother, John Rogers.[88] Early in 1833 Houston left his Cherokee family to seek his fortune in Texas, his immediate purpose being the purchase of land for a New York financier.[89] His arrival in the northern Mexican state was providential for the Texas Cherokees.

The Consultation was monitoring Cherokee activities during the autumn of 1835, but Duwali and Gatunwali convinced several investigators that they were not going to cause trouble. Duwali revealed at a council held in October that after he had gone to San Antonio to talk to Ugartechea, who had tried to enlist their aid against the Texan militia, the Cherokee council had chosen to remain neutral.[90] Meanwhile, General Cós reached and occupied San Antonio in mid-October, and that town was under siege by Texans when the Consultation met in November at San Felipe. A very few days after the assembly convened, its delegates discussed ways of securing and maintaining the neutrality of the immigrant Indians.

On November 13, 1835, fifty-four members of the Consultation pledged "the public faith, on the part of the people of Texas" to give the Cherokees their land. Cancelling all land grants and surveys made in the region, the declaration promised the government's protection to the Cherokees and recognized their claim to lands "north of the San Antonio Road and the Neches, and west of the Angeline and Sabine Rivers."[91] In late November, Houston and two other emissaries were sent to the Cherokees to begin negotiating a treaty. Eleven Cherokee chiefs and one Shawnee chief met with the delegates at

Sims's farm near Nacogdoches. Duwali was not present, and Houston immediately wrote to the chief to assure him that "your land is secured to you. So soon as it is possible you will find Commissioners sent to you, to hold a treaty and fix your lines. I expect that I will be sent to you, and I will then take you the Great paper that was signed by all the council."[92] The Texans promised the Cherokees protection for their land claim and also offered them powder and lead with which to fight the Mexicans.[93]

Duwali and his councillors waited for the Texans to send negotiators. Finally, in December, Houston and two other commissioners were delegated by the Consultation to go to the Cherokees and ensure their neutrality.[94] On February 22, Houston and John Forbes appeared in Duwali's village. Houston had to use his considerable influence with the chiefs to convince them that the treaty would be in their best interests. In vain the commissioners tried to persuade the "beloved man" and his chiefs to exchange their present claim for lands elsewhere. In the end, however, the Cherokees and the Texans compromised.[95]

On February 23, 1836, the compact was signed. The Cherokees and "their associate bands . . . to wit: Shawnee, Delaware, Kickapoo, Quapaw, Choctaw, Biloxi, Ioni, Alabama, Coushatta, Caddo of the Neches, Tahocuttake [*sic*], and Unataqua [*sic*]" were to be given a reservation. Its boundary, which considerably reduced the claim of 1831 to 1833, began at the crossing of the Angelina River and the Bexar Road, followed the Angelina to the first big creek just below the Shawnee village (near present-day Henderson), went up the creek to its source (northeast), then due north to the Sabine, west along the Sabine to its headwaters, then down to the Neches, and down the Neches on the east side to the crossing of the San Antonio Road. The Indians were required to move within these bounds before November 1836 and were to cede any lands presently occupied outside the limits. An agency was to be created within the reservation, and the government of Texas promised to regulate trade with the Indians. Chiefs signing for the Cherokees were "Colonel Boles, Big Mush,

February Eighteen hundred and thirty six, And the First Year of the Provisional Government of Texas. — —

Sam Houston

John Forbes

Witness

his
Fox X Fields
mark
Interpreter

Henry Millard

Joseph Durst

A. Horton

George W. Case

Mathias A. Bingham

G. W. Hockley
Secretary of Commission.

Colonel his X Bowl
mark

his
Big X Mush
mark

his
Samuel X Benge
mark

Oosoota X his
mark

his
Corn X Tassle
mark

his
The X Egg
mark

his
John X Bowl
mark

Tunnetee X his mark

Signature page contained in the Treaty of February 23, 1836; the treaty was signed by Sam Houston and John Forbes for the "Provisional Government of Texas" and by Colonel Bowl (Duwali) and seven other leaders of the Cherokees. Used by permission of the Texas State Library, Austin, Texas.

Samuel Benge, Oosoota, Corn Tassle, The Egg, John Bowls, and Tunnetee," all of whom were Cherokees. Fox Fields, a Cherokee, signed as interpreter. No known chiefs of "associate bands" affixed their marks to the agreement.[96]

The Cherokees negotiated the agreement for several nations which, they claimed, were "Associate Bands." However, no leaders of the "Associate Bands" were present, according to witnesses of the event, and there is no record of a previous intertribal conference binding these nations together. Nevertheless, such may have been the case. Fields had made a union of several of the immigrant tribes in the mid-1820s, and he had often claimed that the Cherokees represented the other tribes by common consent. It is probable that Duwali and the other Cherokees found it expedient to present a united front of all the nations in east Texas. For strength lay in numbers, and more territory could be gained if all of the sedentary nations, both indigenous and immigrant, could be persuaded to share the Cherokees' claim against the Texas Republic.

The Cherokees' council reached a consensus in accepting the 1836 treaty because it promised to give them a permanent home in Texas. During the debates, factional disputes apparently arose, however, over the question of making war on the Comanches and on the Mexicans for the Texans. Some Cherokees must have objected to serving as auxiliaries for the Texans. Despite Houston's persuasive ability and his influence over Duwali, the chief either could not or would not sway the council in the Texas diplomat's favor. In the end the pact did not bind Cherokee warriors to fight for Texas against Mexico or to engage the nation to fight Comanches on the frontier.[97]

Thus, by the terms of the first and last Cherokee treaty with the Republic of Texas, the territory of the immigrant Indian nations was to be circumscribed in Texas just as it had been on the north and east of the Red River. But at last Duwali and his followers saw their territorial demands satisfied. Houston hastened to report the success of his mission, and on February 29 he transmitted the text of the document to Governor Henry Smith for presentation to the Consultation.[98] Earlier, in January, the Consultation had virtually disbanded in anticipation of an invasion of Texas by Santa Ana, and therefore the instrument was never brought up for consideration.[99] With the treaty's conclusion, however, the Cherokees believed that they had at last acquired some measure of legality for their claim. For the time being at least, they would remain neutral in the year of revolution that lay ahead.

«»

4 The Storm: Revolution and Rebellion, 1836–1838

"My people, from the Bigest to the least, have a little dread on their minds"—Bowl to Houston, 11 August 1838 (in Gulick et al., eds., Lamar Papers *2:200–201).*

In the years between 1836 and 1839 the Cherokees witnessed the unfolding of the Texas Revolution of 1836, and a militant faction became partisans in the Mexican effort to reassert control over the region. In these years all the immigrant tribes were courted by both Mexicans and Texans trying to engage them as allies, luring them with promises of title to land the Indians already occupied. On March 1, 1836, the Cherokees' treaty with General Sam Houston was submitted to the convention of militant Texans assembled at Washington-on-the-Brazos, but no action was taken to ratify the document.[1] Meanwhile, the Texas rebellion against Centralism in Mexico rapidly escalated. The convention declared Texas independent of Mexico, wrote a republican constitution, established a temporary government, and raised an army.

Political struggles between Mexico and the insurgents in Texas placed the Cherokees in an increasingly intolerable situation. Their actions during these years have been judged by some as duplicitous and perfidious, but a more objective assessment is that their behavior was culturally consistent; traditional diplomatic maneuvering was complicated by traditional intratribal political factionalism. During these years the Cherokees were dealing with two powerful forces, both sovereign nations with large armies, and the council walked a fine diplomatic line between Texas and Mexico. As each side bargained for their services, the chiefs, not being prescient, were unable to determine which side had the resources to triumph and control Texas. Preserving the lives, homes, and farms of the Cherokee people was the paramount duty of Duwali and the council. During and after the revolution, when the armies and militia of Texas were so close at hand that nervous settlers might call upon these soldiers for protection, the chiefs acted with discretion and appeared neutral in international politics. In reality, however, Duwali was talking with both sides, playing for time, and measuring both the Mexicans and the Texans as adversaries of each other as well as of the Cherokees.

While the aged chief conducted formal negotiations, factionalism, always part of the dynamic of Cherokee politics, again emerged to complicate the scenario. Official policy was directed by Duwali and the council, but it is apparent that some chose not to follow the council's dictates. Though a consensus was no doubt reached in the council, individual Cherokees were not bound to abide by the decision. The inherent factionalism further aggravated the deteriorating situation of the Cherokees in Texas, a fact that must have been perceived by all discerning councillors. Duwali and the council endeavored to keep antagonism against the Texans from escalating into open warfare, which was certain to result in destruction. Nonetheless, some Cherokees insisted upon taking up arms in behalf of Mexico.

The Cherokees listened to at least one, and possibly two, Mexican emissaries who appeared in their councils before and during the Texas Revolution. In mid-February 1836 General Santa Ana noted that the Cherokees "held a solemn promise from the government to give them lands," and that they had helped the government in the past. He posited that if they were placated, they could be "used to good advantage."[2] Within the month the Cherokees were visited by an agent, Eusabio Cortinez, who held a commission from General Cós to raise Indians to fight the Texans.[3] Later, probably in March, Manuel Flores, commissioned as a Mexican agent to the Caddoes, reportedly traveled through east Texas attempting to enlist Indian auxiliaries for the Mexican army.[4]

It is likely that the Cherokees received Cortinez and Flores in councils of their chiefs to which representatives of the Shawnees, Delawares, and Kickapoos had been invited to hear the Mexican offer. In early April Michael Menard, who had been appointed by President Burnet and the Texas Convention as an agent to the tribes "who have migrated from the north," visited in Shawnee, Delaware, and Kickapoo villages about seventy-five miles north of Nacogdoches. His orders were to ascertain the chiefs' collective frame of mind. Chiefs of the three bands alleged that the Cherokees had asked them to fight for the Mexicans.[5]

In March and April 1836 the tide ran against the Texans. Santa Ana's armies had invaded Texas in February, capturing the Alamo on March 6 and Goliad on March 27. General Houston retreated across the Colorado; Washington-on-the-Brazos was abandoned on March 17; and habitations were abandoned along the Brazos. When Houston retreated further eastward, toward the Sabine, the settlements between the Brazos and Sabine were left unprotected, and the Texans in that region abandoned their homes and began moving eastward toward Louisiana. As alarm and confusion and rumor spread like wildfire, settlers around Nacogdoches began moving eastward in the first week of April.[6] An observer noted that everything was left in the flight: "the corn in the crib, the meat in the smokehouse, their poultry, cattle, and furniture."[7]

The Cherokees were undoubtedly alarmed at this strange turn of events, as it appeared that the Texans were about to be trounced by the Mexican army. The Indians' bargaining position had changed; if the Texans lost, the recently signed treaty would be invalid. Obviously, a Mexican alliance would become more attractive under these circumstances. Perceiving this, Houston wrote to Duwali on April 13 to reassure him:

> I am busy and will only say how da do, to you! You will get your land as it was promised in our Treaty, and you and all my

> Red brothers may rest satisfied that I will always hold you by the hand, and look at you as Brothers and treat you as such! . . . Our Army are all well, and in good spirits. In little fight the other day several of the Mexicans were killed, and none of our men hurt. There are not many of the enemy now in the country. . . .[8]

As he watched the settlers fleeing, Duwali may have judged Houston's professions somewhat meretricious, and the council no doubt met to consider a contingency plan of some sort.

The "Runaway Scrape," as the mass exodus before the Mexican invasion has been called, was a difficult time for the Cherokees. As the tide of refugees moved eastward toward Louisiana, the Cherokees became the target of antagonism that under more fortunate circumstances might have been exclusively aimed at the Mexicans. Venturing out from his village, Duwali visited the inhabitants around Nacogdoches, warning them to leave because they were in danger of becoming involved in the war. He pledged the safety of their property while they were gone.[9] Some Americans mistook this as a threat. On April 13 Gatunwali wrote to the Nacogdoches Committee of Safety that the American H. M. Wilson, who had been in the chief's village for several days, had gone to Nacogdoches, along the way spreading a story that the Cherokees had killed some settlers and were planning to attack Americans living near them. Gatunwali reported that the settlers had packed up and vacated their homes because of the tale, and he expressed considerable resentment toward Wilson for having misrepresented the situation. The Cherokees, the chief said, were "all in peace and quietude."[10]

Rumors of imminent attack by Cherokees, Caddoes, Comanches, and other tribes were rife among the American population during the Runaway Scrape. Confusion and fear of the Cherokees' hostility motivated government officials in Nacogdoches to seek protection from U.S. troops stationed in Louisiana. On April 4 a regiment of the U.S. Army, under the command of General E. P. Gaines, had been transferred to Fort Jesup, located in Louisiana between the Sabine River and the town of Natchitoches. After receiving testimony concerning the hostility of the Cherokees and other immigrant and indigenous Texas tribes toward the American residents of east Texas, Gaines perceived a possible danger to the Louisiana frontier. He believed that U.S. Indians might come to help the immigrant Indians in Texas. On April 8 the commander transferred eight companies of the U.S. Seventh Infantry from Fort Gibson, in Indian Territory, to Fort Jesup. When he received information concerning a force of Indians and Mexicans gathered at the Trinity crossing and news of the march of a Mexican division from San Antonio, he ordered five companies of infantry to take up a position on the Sabine River. Here they encountered the Runaway Scrape fugitives fleeing into Louisiana. On April 25 the secretary of war told Gaines that the army should take steps to preserve U.S. territory from Indian depredations, and that he should move no further westward than Nacogdoches. The commander interpreted this as permission to station troops in Texas if necessary. However, after he heard of Texas's victory at San Jacinto on April 21 and of the capture of General Santa Ana, Gaines took no immediate action.[11]

Meanwhile, pressure from both sides may have been pushing the Cherokees into making a decision. Traditionally favoring the building of diplomatic alliances, the Cherokees had maintained a loose partnership with the other immigrant tribes in Texas but had generally been at odds with the Caddoes, Tawakonis, Wacos, and Comanches. Now, for self-preservation, some of them would attempt to join all of the tribes under the Mexican banner and against the Texans. A resident of Nacogdoches noted that Duwali had told him early in April that Indians and Mexicans were beginning to gather near the San Antonio Road crossing on the Trinity River.[12] In mid-April, as a division of Santa Ana's army under General Antonio Gaona advanced from San Antonio toward Nacogdoches, the Cherokees decided to forgo large-scale planting and made an effort to send their women and children to safety.[13] Some of them were getting out the way of the coming battle; others were preparing for action.

In May, Mexican efforts to recruit Indian auxiliaries finally bore fruit, although no Cherokees participated. A council of various Indian nations had taken place in early May, and on May 19 a combined force of Comanches and Caddoes attacked Parker's Fort, a private stockade located at the headwaters of the Navasota River. Members of nine families were killed or captured. Later, attacks were reported by residents of Robertson's colony, near the Brazos River north of Austin's colony.[14] But for the remainder of the summer east Texas was quiet, although rumors of attack by a combined force of Indians continued to circulate, and Mexican agents remained among the Indians, encouraging them to unite and take action.[15]

During the summer of 1836 several parties of Indians, Cherokee diplomats included, traveled to Matamoros to confer with Mexican military officials. In July a group of Cherokees visited General José Urrea, who had replaced General Filisola on July 12 as commander of Mexican troops in that city. These Cherokees agreed not to give the United States reason to interfere on the side of Texas, and Urrea assured them that their lands belonged to them and not to Texas.[16] They also agreed to forestall an attack on the Texans until the Mexican army, regrouped at Matamoros, could reenter Texas and reach the Guadalupe River.[17] Leadership of this delegation remained unnamed; it may have represented the militantly pro-Mexican faction within Duwali's people.

While the Cherokee contingent was in Matamoros, during mid-July, an American military force arrived in Texas en route to Nacogdoches. General Gaines, convinced by Texas leaders that the Mexicans were about to reinvade and that the enemy had arranged for a combination of Indians to attack the settlers, ordered three companies of dragoons and six companies of infantry to move southward from Fort Towson across the Red River into Mexican Texas. After hacking out a supply road through the heart of Cherokee country, the soldiers arrived in Nacogdoches on July 31.[18] A Cherokee council was called at this time, and it can only have had two purposes: to discuss the meaning of this "invasion" by U.S. troops, and to consider a response.[19]

Around August 1, 1836, Texas Indian Agent Menard sent Isadore Pantallion, disguised as a Mexican officer, to Duwali's village. Pantallion was received by a council and spoke directly to the chiefs about their intentions. When asked whether the Cherokees had allied with the Texans, Duwali is said to have grasped a sword purportedly given him by Colonel Ahumada in 1827 and declared, "This shall pass through my heart, before I prove false to my former friends, the Mexicans."[20] Pantallion charged that the chief claimed to have been aligning the immigrant and indigenous tribes to fight the Americans in Texas and that they were now nearly ready, although the Shawnees, Delawares, and Kickapoos had not joined the alliance. The spy also reported that the Cherokees intended to gather the corn and take their cattle to the Sabine; then a force of Indians, which he said was massing on the Trinity River, would attack as soon as the Mexican army returned. Duwali explained that he had sent eight representatives to stay with the Mexican army at Matamoros until the force began to prepare to march into Texas, at which time they were to return as soon as possible. At the end of the interview, Duwali asked Pantallion to explain the presence of the U.S. troops at Nacogdoches. When the spy commented that the United States claimed its boundary as the Neches River, rather than the Red and the Sabine, Duwali is said to have remarked that this was "just like Americans, always stealing piece by piece."[21]

It is possible that Duwali made an exaggerated statement for the benefit of a presumed Mexican officer. With Texas military forces still under arms and in the vicinity, with American forces in Nacogdoches and also poised on the Sabine a few days march away, and with Mexican forces in disarray at Matamoros, it would have been uncharacteristically rash of the chief to assume an overtly martial stance. But for a few words, by making threats against the Texans, he might increase the Cherokees' standing with the Mexicans, whose protection they might need in the future. Unfortunately for the chief, the pro-Mexican faction among the Cherokees was turning braggadocio into fact. It is difficult to assess the nature of the council's debate at this point. With a militant faction growing and negotiating with other Indians and with Mexicans, Duwali would have been hard pressed to maintain a consensus for neutrality. At this time the chief himself seemed to have been leaning toward the pro-Mexican position, but he and his advisors must have known that under the circumstances they could scarcely afford to show a hostile attitude toward Texans.

Agent Menard, meanwhile, sojourned among the Shawnees, ferreting out information about the Cherokees. He informed Houston that in his opinion the Shawnees, Delawares, and Kickapoos were inclined to keep out of the fight, but that the Cherokees, Biloxis, Choctaws, Alabamas, and Caddoes appeared to be ready to march and reportedly had allied with the Comanches, Wacos, and Tawakonis to attack within the month.[22] The story was corroborated by Juan Basques, who had been in an Ioni village on the Neches in August. According to Basques, on August 23 two Cherokees, Fox [Fields] and Etoi, had come in for a conference; then, on August 28, the ubiquitous Eusabio Cortinez arrived in the Ioni town and announced that all of the Indians were expected to meet at Duwali's village the next day to plan an attack on Nacogdoches.[23]

Menard's news of the contemplated alliance galvanized Houston into action. From Nacogdoches, where he was campaigning for the presidency of the Republic of Texas, he hastily wrote to General Gaines, advising him that Cherokees had been to Matamoros to treat with the Mexicans and had come back with the story that the "Indians of the prairies" were about to attack. The general suggested that Gaines reinforce the American troops in Nacogdoches.[24] Next, although he had given up active command of the Texas army on May 5 due to a wound received at San Jacinto, on August 28 he issued a proclamation calling for several communities to raise a militia in defense.[25]

The militant Cherokees had anticipated the swift return of the Mexican army, but their hopes were dashed when the invasion never materialized. Shortly thereafter, when fears were allayed, President Houston warned the militia and officers of the regular Texas army not to go into the Indians' territory or initiate any violence.[26] The pro-Mexican faction apparently had second thoughts about attacking Nacogdoches without the support of a Mexican army, and they were possibly intimidated by the presence of Gaines's U.S. troops and by the activities of assorted militia companies.[27]

In September 1836 the Cherokees entertained an intriguing proposal from Houston, who was elected president of the republic on September 5 and was now officially in charge of its Indian affairs. On September 1 a party of Cherokees appeared in Nacogdoches, presumably to see Houston, but also to trade with the inhabitants.[28] By the middle of the month the Cherokees agreed to provide a company of twenty-five rangers to patrol the country from the Sabine River to the Comanche crossing on the Trinity River, west of the Cherokees' towns. For their services the Indian rangers were to receive $10 per month, and their captain was to receive $20 per month. The object of the corps was to protect the frontier from the Comanches. As an added bonus the Cherokees were to be allowed to keep all of the spoils.[29] These pro-Texas Cherokees would now press Duwali to align the people with Houston's forces.

A desperate Duwali must have entertained thoughts of saving the situation and protecting his people's interests by aligning with the Texans. Surely the debates in the Cherokee council must have been heated. Based on past performance, there were three possible opinions on the course that should now be followed. A younger group probably wanted to pursue an immediate war with Texas; another, no doubt, wanted to wait for the arrival of the Mexican army before taking up arms; and another, possibly led by Duwali, now argued in favor of accepting Houston's friendship and hoping for fair treatment from the Texans, who appeared to have won the contest over political control of the former Mexican state. That various groups were withdrawing and taking independent action became evident during the next few months.

Anticipating trouble, Duwali had moved his own village from a creek near the Sabine to a new location near the Neches Saline, in the southwestern corner of present Smith County. This move was made after the Runaway Scrape, and Duwali soon operated a thriving business selling salt. It is reasonable to speculate that the purpose of shifting the village location to the southwest was to lessen its proximity to U.S. troops massed on the Sabine at Fort Jesup. In September Houston appointed

Martin Lacy as trader to the Cherokees; Lacy was directed to take over the Saline, from which he was to provide Duwali six bushels of salt per month. The site was forty miles from Nacogdoches but still within the territory claimed by the Cherokees and accorded them in Houston's 1836 treaty. This notwithstanding, the government confiscated the Saline.[30] Because it was the source of a valuable commodity, the site was not to be left for the Indians' exclusive use.

Some Cherokees who preferred to maintain a pro-Mexican stance went to Matamoros in December 1836. Here they conferred with General Juan Amador, commander in chief of the Mexican army based at the mouth of the Rio Grande. According to Anthony Butler, former U.S. minister to Mexico, who was in Matamoros at this time and witnessed several meetings between the Indians and the general, these Cherokees had agreed to attack all along the northern frontier in the early spring. The Mexicans promised to attack from the west at the same time.[31]

Duwali and Houston continued to correspond throughout the winter, the president diligently trying to enlist the Indians as military allies. Finally, the chief agreed to serve as an emissary to the Comanches for the republic. In March 1837 the aged chief went out on an extended visit to the "Prairie Indians," a large body of whom were said to be gathered at the three forks of the Trinity.[32] He spent most of March and all of April on the trails between the villages and camps of many different tribes.[33]

While Duwali was on his diplomatic mission for Texas, the pro-Mexican Cherokees took further measures to promote their own cause. Early in March Eusabio Cortinez and Manuel Flores were again in the Nacogdoches area working among the Indians, as was Vicente Cordova, a Nacogdoches resident and advocate of a Mexican Texas.[34] Gatunwali busily tried to keep the Cherokees out of the way of these individuals. He was assisted by William Goyens, a free black man who resided in Nacogdoches and often served as an interpreter and messenger for the Cherokees. Despite their efforts, some of the warriors joined Cortinez's party.[35] In late July Cortinez and eight or ten Cherokees were attacked and killed by Comanches in a battle near Matamoros.[36]

Duwali returned around May 1, 1837, and within a few days he called a council of the headmen of all the Cherokee villages. In a lengthy speech he reported to them that he had been to see the Caddoes, Ionis, Taovayas, Tawakonis, Wacos, and Kichais, all of whom said that they were no longer seeking vengeance for wrongs done by the Texans and that they were ready to hold a council to talk of peace. Duwali reported that he had tentatively arranged for a council of all of these tribes to be held in mid-June. Continuing with his report, he said that he had gone out to find Comanches but found only eight camps. Each had agreed to come to the conference, but, in his opinion, they were not seriously interested in making peace. Then the chief had traveled north to the Wichitas living on the Red River, but they refused to listen to him. With them and with the Comanches, he said, he favored war, and he asked the assemblage to support his viewpoint.[37]

As the meeting concluded, the aged chief announced that he was going to send Gatunwali to conduct the upcoming conference. The purpose of this move is not immediately clear. Duwali may simply have been debilitated by his recent travels, or the Cherokees' council may have been relieving him of part of the diplomatic role that he had assumed following the Fredonian affair of 1827. Here Gatunwali appears to have been resuming the role of diplomat. Stating that he did not want to make the journey, Duwali added that he would go if Houston insisted. He also warned Houston not to send any representatives to this first council, but suggested that Texans would be welcome to attend a second meeting to be held later on the Sabine.[38] After attending this initial council, William Goyens relayed a message from Houston that the president would like the chiefs to come to the city of Houston to confer with him. In reply, the council asked Goyens to inform Houston of the upcoming conferences and to tell him that the chiefs preferred to postpone a trip to the capital until after the first meeting.[39]

A few weeks later Duwali received word from a band of Comanches that they would like to hold a talk. The chief informed the authorities in Nacogdoches, because the Comanches had indicated a desire to establish a trade with both the Americans and the Cherokees.[40] Under the pro-Texas Cherokees' agreement with the Texas Republic, they were supposed to be fighting the nomadic tribes to the west rather than trading with them. When Houston received information about this new development, he directed General Rusk to encourage the Cherokees, Shawnees, Kickapoos, Coushattas, Choctaws, and Biloxis to begin operations against the Comanches and others.[41]

Houston then decided it would be wise to make an appearance in Nacogdoches to attend the second council that was supposed to be held in June on the Sabine. He ordered Rusk to tell the chiefs of the Cherokees, Shawnees, Delawares, Biloxis, Choctaws, and Kickapoos to meet with him in Nacogdoches on June 30. Around the middle of the month he engaged a guide and set out on horseback from Houston, but the presidential guide managed to lose his way, the horses went lame, and a disgusted Houston arrived in Nacogdoches around the first of July.[42] He immediately sent word to Duwali to come to Nacogdoches in four days, telling the chief to bring with him his copy of the 1836 treaty and also to bring the Kickapoo, Caddo, and Delaware leaders.[43] This meeting probably never transpired, given Duwali's temporarily tenuous position with his people. In mid-July a worried president offered the chief a munificent $2,000 a year to take the field for Texas against hostile tribes, or $1,000 a year if he did not take the field but only aligned with Texas.[44] There is no record that the Cherokees accepted.

The Cherokees' treaty, which had been submitted to the Senate of the Texas Republic on December 20, 1836, was under investigation during the summer of 1837. Soon after becoming the new nation's chief executive, Houston inaugurated an Indian policy. To encourage friendship with the indigenous and immigrant tribes, he sent commissioners to the Anadarkos, Ionis, Kichais, Wacos, Taovayas, and Tawakonis.[45] In May 1837 the Senate appointed a three-man committee to study the Indian situation and to make recommendations on the validity of Duwali's 1836 agreement with Houston.[46] On October 12 Senators Isaac W. Burton, of Nacogdoches, Sterling C. Robertson, of Milam, and Thomas Jefferson Green, of Bexar, reported on all of the tribes, their cultural characteristics, their numbers, and their places of residence.

Information on the Cherokees occupied nearly half of the committee's attention, and the three were perceptive in noticing that the Cherokees had two chiefs whose duties were separate: "Their war chief is called Bowles, their Civil Chief is called Big Mush," the report noted. It also implied, but did not present proof, that the Cherokees had made a treaty of military alliance with the Comanches, and the legislators made the menacing observation that "The Cherokees in the event of war would feel the Horros [*sic*] of invasion in a degree very nearly equal to the whites as their Squaws and Children never leave their farms. . . . They would have no strongholds, no interminable thickets, or swamps to retire to, but would be forced to give battle or fly to the prairies."[47]

Immediately following this came the committee's evaluation of the agreements made between the Cherokees and the Mexican government and with the Consultation in 1835. In their opinion, no rights were given the Indians by the Mexicans, and the Consultation's Declaration was invalid because it was based upon the false assumption that the Cherokees held vested rights given by the Mexican government. The committee branded the Cherokees "the most savage and ruthless of our frontier enemies" and held that the 1826 Mexican grant to David G. Burnet was evidence that the Mexican republic had not intended the land for the Indians. And, finally, the three offered a resolution rejecting Duwali's and Houston's Treaty of 1836.[48]

Augmenting Houston's policy of making treaties to pacify the frontier, the committee recommended ratification of a pact recently concluded with the Anadarkos and Ionis by Texas Indian Commissioners Thomas Jefferson Rusk and Kelsey Douglas. It also recommended that the president appoint commissioners to conclude a treaty with the Comanches. These moves by the president and the committee would seem to indicate that the Cherokees were on the verge of diplomatic isolation. They were no longer acting as paid rangers against the hostile nations or as leaders of so-called "Associate Bands," which had presumably included the Anadarkos, Ionis, and Kichais. On December 16, 1837, the Senate voted to nullify the Cherokee treaty.[49] Ratification of the Anadarko-Ioni treaty separated the Cherokees from two of their allies, if only on paper.

How the Cherokee council received the Texas Senate's decision can only be surmised, but it is not unreasonable to suppose that many of them were angered by the outcome. It may be that the failure of the treaty encouraged the pro-Mexican faction among the Cherokees to push Duwali into taking steps to tie his people's fortunes to those of the Mexicans once again. Perhaps Duwali realized that even Houston's forceful personality could not overcome the Texans' enmity toward the Cherokees or prevent a continuing loss of tribal land.

Americans were moving into the east Texas region in ever-increasing numbers. As far back as October 1835, under the Mexican regime, a total of 101 titles had been issued within the borders of land claimed by the Cherokees. Between October 27, 1835, and October 1, 1837, the land offices had been closed, but after they reopened, several hundred more titles were registered.[50] In May 1838 Houston noted in an address to the Texas Senate:

> The Indian lands are forbidden fruit in the midst of the garden; their blooming peach trees, their snug cabins, their well-cultivated fields, and their lowing herds excite the speculators, whose cupidity, reckless of the consequences which would ensue to the country, by goading the Indians to desperation, are willing to hazard everything that is connected to the safety, prosperity, and honor of the country.[51]

Duwali was disgruntled because of Houston's inability to control the situation. The chief visited the president in Houston in early April 1838, and after the conference he is said to have complained that he had given Houston his daughter for a wife and had helped make him a "big chief" in the Cherokee nation, but that now Houston was "no longer a Cherokee but 'the Great Father' of the white men."[52] On June 14 the Cherokees hosted a council of chiefs of the Delawares, Kickapoos, and Coushattas, and all expressed their disappointment that Texas did not intend to fulfill Houston's promises.[53]

Shortly thereafter, Duwali wrote to the Cherokees in Indian Territory and asked for reinforcements. Specifically, he sent word to Tahchee (Dutch), the same Cherokee headman who had resided in Texas between 1828 and 1831, and whose village in 1838 was located at the confluence of the Canadian and Arkansas rivers approximately equidistant from Fort Gibson and Fort Smith.[54] Duwali asked Tahchee to persuade the national council to send warriors to Texas and to bring the Creeks and Seminoles to fight with them, promising that if they conquered Texas, General Vicente Filisola would give them permanent possession of the region.[55] The Western Cherokee council debated Duwali's request but decided against helping the Cherokees in Texas. Furthermore, they ordered "that none of their young men should leave" for Texas.[56] At this point, the Western Cherokees determined it would not have been good diplomatic policy to aid in an uprising taking place in another nation. On December 29, 1835, in the Treaty of New Echota, the Eastern Cherokees had agreed to remove west of the Mississippi within two years of the date of the ratification of the treaty, which the U.S. Senate accomplished on May 23, 1836. In 1837 nearly a thousand emigrants had arrived in present-day eastern Oklahoma on land reserved to the Western Cherokees in 1828, and in the summer and fall of 1838 the stream became a flood as the majority of the eastern portion of the Cherokee nation were forcibly removed to the Western Cherokees reservation.[57] Cherokees in Texas would receive no support from their kinsmen in Indian Territory.

The Texas Cherokees faced a deadly serious diplomatic situation. The long-awaited Mexican invasion was not forthcoming, and Texas had reneged on the 1836 treaty. Duwali and the councillors were faced with a fateful decision. Should they continue in the present vein, hardships at the hands of the Texans were a certainty. Located on the best lands in Texas, they were prime targets, at the very least, for removal to less-habitable lands elsewhere in the Texas Republic. A

Mexican alliance, should it assist in achieving a successful reinvasion of Texas, might offer a more secure future. Duwali and his councillors were apparently swayed to the militants' viewpoint, and the Cherokees seriously considered becoming allies of the Mexicans.

There may have been one or more Mexican agents working among the Texas Indians in the early months of 1838. In the autumn of 1837 the Mexican army had been planning an attack on Texas for the following spring and summer, and in late May 1838 General José Urrea, Filisola's successor as commander of the Mexican army, sent an Indian commissioner from Matamoros to Texas.[58] Julian Pedro Miracle's mission was to secure Indian auxiliaries for the coming fight. His orders were twofold. First, upon reaching Texas he was to call a council of all of the "captains of friendly Indians of Texas" to ask them to "take up arms in defense of the integrity of the Mexican territory in Texas."[59] The Indians were to be given powder, lead, and tobacco, and they were to take the field immediately. He was also to promise them that "as soon as the campaign is over, they will be able to proceed to Mexico, to pay their respects to the Supreme Government, who will send a commissioner to give each possession of the land they are entitled to."[60] Miracle's second instruction involved raising troops and provisions among the Mexican Texans, in anticipation of a reinvasion.[61] The agent left Matamoros on May 29 with a force consisting of seventy-two Mexicans, thirty-four soldiers, and twenty Cherokees and Caddoes. By June 20 Miracle's company reached the San Antonio River, where they met briefly with Manuel Flores.

By July 5 the entourage had traveled as far as the Trinity River, and on that day Vicente Cordova arrived to confer with Miracle. Cordova, a former alcalde and judge under the Mexican regime, was organizing the Mexican Texans of Nacogdoches for the operation. Three days later, Duwali visited the camp and left a Cherokee guide to bring the company to his village. They arrived on July 9, and the Cherokees hid Miracle and his troupe until the twentieth, when chiefs of the Cherokees, Delawares, and Shawnees gathered with Cordova and a group of Nacogdochians to listen to Miracle's offer.[62] In the course of this meeting the Shawnees strenuously objected to beginning the operation before the arrival of the Mexican army, but Duwali and the Cherokees accepted the offer. They also agreed to come immediately to the aid of the Mexican Texans if the plan were accidentally revealed before the invasion.[63] The agent continued his journey, meeting with the Kickapoos, Chickasaws, Caddoes, Wacos, Kichais, and Tawakonis during the latter part of July.[64] In early August, however, Miracle's party was discovered by a band of Nacogdochians searching for stolen livestock, and word of his activities was quickly carried to the Texas authorities.[65]

Meanwhile, militant Cherokees gathered with an armed contingent of approximately six hundred Mexican Texans and Indians who were rallying with Vicente Cordova on the Angelina River northwest of Nacogdoches. Cordova and his followers soon camped a few miles from Duwali's village.[66] President Houston had definite misgivings about what the Cherokees were planning to do, and he plainly suspected that some of them might be in league with the rebels. On August 10 he allowed General Thomas Jefferson Rusk, commander of the Texas militia, to raise the militia and station some of them at the lower crossing of the Angelina River.[67] Over the next few days Houston, in Nacogdoches, and Rusk, in the field, reinforced various defensive positions and tried to disengage the Cherokees from the rebels.

Houston was determined to keep his Indian kinsmen out of the fight if there was to be one. He ordered Rusk, who was camped at the San Antonio Road crossing of the Angelina, to avoid a confrontation by staying on the east side of the river, outside the Indians' claim. When Rusk reported that he had communicated with Duwali and that the chief, too, appeared to want to avoid bloodshed, Houston commended Rusk for treating the Indians kindly.[68] The president appeared to be worried about what Rusk would do to the Cherokees in the event the two forces joined in battle.

Duwali and Gatunwali both received worried pleas from the chief executive on August 10 and 11. Encouraging them to

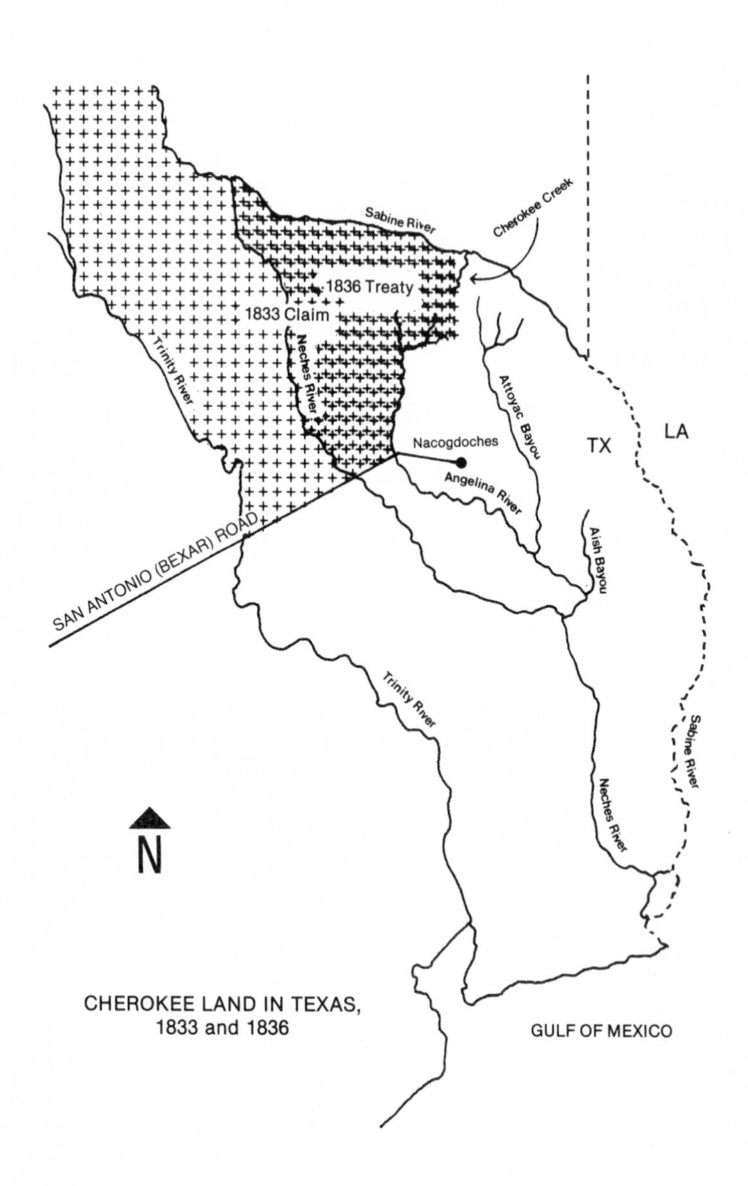

CHEROKEE LAND IN TEXAS,
1833 and 1836

"Stand by the treaty," he reassured them that the boundary line would soon be surveyed around the Cherokees' reserve and that he would "never lie to that treaty while I live and it will stand as long as good men live and water runs."[69] The volatile situation so distressed Houston that he also sent word to Colonel R. B. Many, U.S. commander at Fort Jessup, Louisiana, that the Texans needed reinforcements and ordnance.[70]

Despite Houston's reassurances, Duwali remained concerned about Rusk's presence on the Angelina. On the eleventh he replied to Houston that "my people from the Bigest to the least have a little dread on their minds" because of a visit from a Biloxi man, who said that he had "heard white men threaten to kill the Indians." The chief asked Houston to send him some news as soon as possible.[71] Houston responded apologetically on the twelfth: "My brother: Before the surveyer could get time to run the line, the fuss began . . . I have given an order that no families or children of Indians shall be disturbed or have trouble, but that they shall be protected and even the Mexican families' property may not be troubled."[72] To Rusk, Houston wrote that he must suppress all firing in camp, keep his lines intact, listen for the "Indian yell," and be aware that this enemy would attack at night and at several places.[73] The president was evidently convinced that an attack would come, even if the Cherokees declined to take part. The next day he ordered Rusk to send scouts up the Angelina to discover any enemy activity, and his words reflected his growing doubt about the Cherokees' intentions: "If the Bowl means to compromise with the enemy—you accept such terms as will give honorable peace to the country."[74]

Knowing Houston's feelings for the Cherokees, Rusk communicated with Duwali, reprimanding him for harboring renegade Mexicans in his villages and warning the chief that the Texans were soon going to march through Cherokee country in pursuit of the rebels. The general also sent two men to visit the Cherokees, but Duwali refused to see any white man other than Peter Ellis Bean, who, it seems, was in league with Cordova.[75] But in communications with Houston, Rusk expressed his own views, noting ominously that Duwali "must know a hostile force camped in his area gives us leave to follow them there," and complaining that he wished "this infernal question of war or peace with the Cherokees was settled, as it embarrasses my operations greatly."[76] Rusk was in a hurry to be on the march after the rebels, and he wanted Houston to be aware of the urgency of the mission.

Houston, too, was anxious for the business to be settled, preferably without harm to his Cherokee kinsmen. He wrote to Duwali on the fourteenth, this time speaking frankly about Duwali's alleged collusion with the Mexicans: "My brother: I hear the enemy are in your village—they must not stay there. 2000 men on Red River are under arms and U.S. cannons will come from the Sabine. In ten days we will have over 1000 men here. I hope to the Great Spirit that my Red Brother will not make war or join our enemies."[77] The president correctly perceived that the spectre of battle with U.S. troops would frighten Duwali and the other chiefs into abandoning Cordova. But the warning came too late to stop Rusk; despite Houston's orders to the contrary, the Texas commander took his militia across the Angelina and marched to Duwali's town. There, Texas scouts discovered that the Mexicans had abandoned their camp, but the rebels were quickly located two miles from the Cherokee village.[78]

Proximity to the Texas militia apparently accentuated or brought once again to the fore the division of opinion in the Cherokees' council. On August 15 Gatunwali and nine other chiefs came to Rusk's camp to declare their peaceful intentions.[79] This chief and his entourage may have been serving in a bona fide diplomatic capacity, representing a consensus which wanted peace with the Texans and had decided to try to salvage something from the situation by acting on their own to restore amicable relations. After talking with John Durst, an agent sent by Rusk, Duwali also agreed to delay action until another meeting could be held with the Texans.[80] But before this conference transpired, Cordova decided to cancel the operation for the time being.[81]

Over the next two days, most of the rebels deserted Cordova and returned to their homes in and around Nacogdoches. On August 18 Houston disbanded most of the Texas militia.[82] The rebel leader gathered his few remaining followers, minus two who were sent by Duwali to Houston as captives, and retreated into the heavily wooded areas around the headwaters of the Trinity River, and Rusk judged it useless to pursue them.[83] On August 26 Houston, in a move no doubt calculated to pacify the Cherokees and to smooth over any ill will created by Rusk, directed the general to take steps to have the Cherokees' boundary surveyed, despite the treaty's rejection by the Texas Senate a year earlier.[84]

For the next month the Cherokees came under intense scrutiny by Texas, and it appeared from activities within and without the nation that another uprising might be forthcoming. On August 20 Julian Pedro Miracle, the Mexican agent who had come to Texas earlier in the year, was killed in a skirmish in the Cross Timbers near the Red River, where he may have been mustering Indian auxiliaries. Taken from his body were his instructions from General Filisola and his diary, which revealed Cordova's and Flores's activities and successes among the immigrant and indigenous Indians.[85] Many Texans immediately inferred from Miracle's presence on the Red River that he had been on his way to Arkansas to engage various Indian nations in an assault on Texas.[86] Rumors spread that Manuel Flores had returned from Matamoros with commissions for Cordova and others, that Duwali and Gatunwali were about to be deposed as chiefs, that parties of Ionis, Anadarkos, Kichais, and Caddoes had been seen in Cherokee villages, and that a substantial force of Mexicans and Indians was assembling on the Sabine River north of Nacogdoches.[87]

During this period Rusk ascertained that the Cherokees were selling their stock and storing provisions in the cane brakes, and that parties of Cherokees were stockpiling powder, lead, and whiskey.[88] Another Texas emissary to the Cherokees, C. H. Sims, reported to Rusk that when he recently visited Duwali's village the chief had packed his belongings and all the Indians appeared to be leaving. A militia captain sent to Gatunwali's village reported that all of the houses were vacant and that the Indians had left with their belongings.[89] The Indians apparently had knowledge that the fighting would continue, and in October the rebel-Indian force resumed their activities.

Early in October 1838 Mexican Texans and Indians, presumably led by Cordova or Flores, or both, began military operations against the frontier settlements. On October 5 an attack was made on the Killoughs, a large family living on a creek just inside the Cherokee claim, south of the Neches Saline. This assault, which resulted in the death of eighteen members of the family, was perpetrated by a combined force of Shawnees and Biloxis. Cherokees, however, were implicated by the survivors.[90] A short time later an attack followed on Fort Houston, on the Trinity River two miles west of present-day Palestine.[91] In earlier months, Fort Houston had been a mustering point for Texas militia, and several companies of militia remained there. It was later alleged by a survivor of the "Killough massacre" that about forty-five Cherokees were involved in plans for attacks on the frontier.[92]

After the October raids Rusk again mobilized east Texas militia, and with a force of over two hundred men marched westward through the Cherokee nation to Fort Houston. An agitated Duwali wrote to Rusk to inform him that he was leaving because of threats by Mexicans and Indians against him, and Gatunwali wrote to inform the general that the Mexican-Indian force was camped at the Kickapoos' village, which lay northwest of the Cherokees.[93] The Texas commander quick-marched his troops to the Kickapoos' village and engaged in battle with a force of Kickapoos, Mexicans, Caddoes, Coushattas, and Kichais on October 16, killing eleven of them. Included among the dead was one Cherokee, known as Tail.[94] After the battle, which has since been known as the "Kickapoo War," Rusk immediately sent word to Duwali that he had "punished" the Mexicans and Indians and that at least one Cherokee had been with them. Warning Duwali to keep his young men away from the Mexicans, he advised the chief to come to Nacogdoches with Gatunwali and hold a talk.[95] But by this time Houston had taken steps to mollify the Cherokees.

That the chief executive was concerned about the safety of

the frontier was evident. He ordered Rusk to have the Cherokees' boundary line marked, noting:

> If it is not immediately done, all future calamaties must be attributed to its omission. I am satisfied if it is not done there will be another runaway scrape and Eastern Texas will be desolated. . . . If it is not done an Indian war may ensue which may cost more blood and treasure than ought to purchase twenty such Indian countries.[96]

Shortly thereafter, Duwali admitted Alexander Horton, a surveyor, into the nation. Horton had been appointed on October 10 by the president, and he was commanded to finish the job within twenty days. Duwali provided men to guard the surveying party.[97] Horton proceeded to run the line, despite his feeling that "designing persons in the neighborhood of Nacogdoches were determined to involve the country in a general Indian war." On October 11 he took a crew of fifty men, including sixteen Cherokees, into the field; they stayed out during the "Kickapoo War" and finished the survey in nineteen days. In his report to Houston, Horton noted that he had constantly to reassure Duwali that the Cherokees would be protected from attack by whites in east Texas.[98] At the conclusion of the task, Horton reported that the Cherokees appeared to be satisfied now that their property line had been demarcated.

Surrounded by a growing number of American settlers clamoring for good farmland and grazing land, embroiled in the machinations of the Mexicans for a reinvasion of the region, and caught up in the struggle of Mexicans with Texans for political control of the region, the Cherokees were, as General Rusk would later so aptly describe the situation, "between two fires." It was no doubt increasingly obvious to Duwali and the other chiefs that their situation in east Texas was becoming more and more untenable. The dictates of Cherokee diplomatic tradition had led them to talk with both sides, to negotiate for the most advantageous position. But the tradition of factionalism, so functional a part of traditional Cherokee internal politics, had led to division. Adherents of a pro-Mexican stance and adherents of a pro-Texas policy followed their own paths while Duwali and the council vainly tried to keep the people on a neutral course until the elders could determine which political entity would finally achieve sovereignty over Texas. Unfortunately, the chiefs could only attempt to persuade all to reach a consensus; they had no coercive authority over factions. Thus the coming year would hold few bright moments for the Western Cherokees in Texas.

«»

5

"Between Two Fires": War and Removal, 1839–1840

"Chief Bowles displayed great courage in these battles. In the second engagement he remained on the field on horseback, wearing a military hat, silk vest, and handsone sword and sash which had been presented to him by President Houston. He was a magnificent picture of barbaric manhood and was very conspicuous during the whole battle, being the last to leave the field when the Indians retreated. His horse, however, was now disabled, and he dismounted, after having been wounded himself. As he walked away he was shot in the back and fell. Then, as he sat up with his face toward us, I started toward him with a view to secure his surrender. At the same time my captain, Bob Smith, with a pistol in his hand, ran toward him from farther down the line. We reached him at the same instant, and realizing what was imminent, I called, 'Captain, don't shoot him.' But he fired, striking Bowles in the head, and killing him instantly"—John Hunter Reagan, eyewitness to Duwali's death, July 1839 (in Reagan, Memoirs, *ed. Walter F. McCaleb, pp. 34–35).*

In the years preceding the removal war of 1839 the Texas Cherokees followed the dictates of diplomatic tradition to negotiate with both sides for an advantageous position. But the tradition of factionalism worked in the opposite direction, creating disunity. In 1839, as individual Cherokees continued to fight in behalf of Mexico, all of Duwali's people would endure punishment administered by the army of the Republic of Texas.

After the abortive Cordova affair and the "Kickapoo War" of 1838, the Cherokees and other tribes took measures for self-defense. The pro-Mexican faction again entertained emissaries from Matamoros, despite the expulsion by General Rusk's militia in November of a large number of Caddoes from Texas into U.S. territory.[1] By mid-December there were 250 Cherokee and Delaware warriors based near the village of

Delaware chief Harris, and Duwali was reportedly trying to engage the Shawnees in an attack on Nacogdoches.[2] The Indians made no move to attack, however, and Rusk held his men in check. By spring, affairs had calmed.

A political turn of events in the Texas Republic did not bode well for the Cherokees. Houston's term as chief executive was drawing to an end; Mirabeau Buonaparte Lamar, man of letters and inveterate enemy of Cherokees, had been elected to the presidency in September. A native Georgian, Lamar had served as secretary to Governor George M. Troup from 1823 to 1826. Subsequently, he became a newspaper publisher and state senator at a time when the state of Georgia was attempting to rid itself of the Cherokees. In 1835 he came to Texas for his health. Arriving just in time to participate in the Texas Revolution, he served in the battle at San Jacinto in 1836 and was commissioned a colonel on the battlefield. After a brief and unsuccessful period as major general and commander of the Texas Army, he retired to civilian life. Elected as Houston's vice president, he was promoted for the presidency by Houston's enemies.[3] President Lamar was inaugurated on December 10, 1838, and in his first policy statement indicated that the removal of the Western Cherokees from Texas was a goal he intended to pursue.[4] In the next few months Duwali, Gatunwali, and their councillors were pressured by Texas to give up their homes and leave Texas.

Mexican officials were very interested in continuing to promote an Indian alliance against Texas. In the later months of 1838 Mexico had become involved in a war with France, and various Mexican ports had been bombarded and invaded. General Santa Ana was organizing the army to defend the east coast, and Mexican troops at Matamoros were enjoined from reentering Texas. With his command ordered to remain at Matamoros, General Valentin Canalizo fixed on the idea of creating an Indian alliance as a holding action against Texas until his army could reconquer the province. In the early months of 1839 Canalizo's agent in Texas, Vicente Cordova, was ranging the frontier and visiting various tribes.[5] In February of that year Canalizo commissioned Manuel Flores to return to Texas, and in March Flores began his journey in the company of thirteen Mexican rangers and eleven Indian auxiliaries. Cordova, meanwhile, was asked by Canalizo to once again enlist the aid of "the friendly tribes of Indians" to meet with Flores and follow his instructions.[6]

Flores's orders were to unite the tribes and use them as auxiliaries to harass the Texas "colonists," preventing them from consolidating their recent victory at San Jacinto. Canalizo's directive involved two strategies. The first was to cut off Texas's access to both American and Mexican markets by forming a semicircular line of defense from the Red River on the northeast to the coast on the south. The second was to institute guerilla warfare. The Indians were directed "not to cease to harass the enemy for a single day—to burn their habitations, to lay waste their fields, and to prevent them from assembling in great numbers, by rapid and well-concerted movements, so as to draw their attention in every direction, and not to offer to them any determinate object at which to strike. . . ."[7] For their trouble, the tribes were to "be secured in the peaceable possession of your lands."[8] Canalizo sent letters with Flores for chiefs of the Caddoes, Kickapoos, Shawnees, and other tribes, as well as for Gatunwali and Duwali of the Cherokees.[9]

By late spring 1839, affairs in east Texas were relatively calm. In April Duwali adopted an ingratiating stance toward Texas, a wise diplomatic maneuver under the circumstances. The chief told Rusk that he had been out to see the hostile tribes and had asked for peace, to which, he said, they had agreed. The chief added that he had recently seen Cordova but had rejected his overtures and sent the agent away.[10] Such a report to the commander of Texas forces was certainly politic, but it fell short of an accurate appraisal of recent events.

That the Cherokees were suffering under a lack of consensus is probable. Some, Duwali in particular, were influenced by Houston to believe that the Republic of Texas would eventually honor the 1836 treaty. Others, probably the younger men, preferred to fight on the Mexican side in hopes of ridding Texas of Anglo-Americans. This situation of internal division had ample precedent in the 1827 Fredonian affair and in the 1838 Cordova uprising, though in neither case had it succeeded. While Duwali and the older headmen conducted talks with Texans and Mexicans, younger men chose to go into battle alongside Mexicans and other Indians who opposed the conciliatory tactics of the peace chiefs. That the Cherokee political organization was out of equilibrium, with a militant faction following an independent course, became evident in the spring of 1839 as Texas insisted that the Indians leave the country. Because of the middle course taken by Duwali and the council, the Texans thought Duwali was lying, or at least masking his real intentions.

Mexican agent Flores and his contingent came up from Matamoros in April, and by May he was in Texas. On May 17 rangers under Lieutenant James O. Rice discovered, attacked, and routed Flores's men on the San Gabriel River, twenty-five miles north of present-day Austin. Unfortunately, the rangers captured a packet of letters containing correspondence between Canalizo, Flores, and Cordova as well as Canalizo's letters to the various immigrant chiefs. The captured documents were quickly sent to General Edward Burleson, commander of the First Regiment of Texas Infantry, and on to Albert Sidney Johnston, Texas secretary of war.[11]

For the future of the Texas Cherokees, the impact of this revelation cannot be overstated. Although Flores never completed his mission and, therefore, Duwali and Gatunwali may not have ever received Canalizo's circular, President Lamar lost no time in taking advantage of the situation to counter what he perceived to be danger of another Mexican foray against the infant republic. In his view, the Cherokees were implicated as conspirators, working as the advance guard of invasion.[12]

In May, after the discovery of Flores's papers, Lamar sent an armed force under Major B. C. Waters to occupy the Neches Saline, inside the Cherokees' claim. Duwali suspected that the purpose of this advance might be to prevent cooperation among the tribes supposedly aligned with Mexico.[13] When the chief threatened Waters with forceful resistance, the commander prudently elected to set up his headquarters out of Cherokee territory, on the Neches. Duwali complained to General Rusk that the presence of Waters's troops "has alarmed our women and children very much," and pointed out that he had kept his word in talking to the "wild tribes" for the general.[14] Later in May Duwali received from President Lamar a communication amounting to an ultimatum for the Cherokees' council to consider. Lamar's letter was carefully borne to Duwali's village by Martin Lacey, the Texas Indian agent, accompanied by two Nacogdoches militiamen, Dr. W. G. W. Jowers and John H. Reagan.[15]

Duwali received the delegation cordially, and an interpreter translated the letter. Not surprisingly, the president began by denying the Cherokees' right to live in Texas as a nation within a nation. Stating that the Indians could not claim any authority under a treaty ruled illegitimate, he pointed out that it was not within their power to order Major Waters from the Saline. Adding that it would be "wise in you to say to the Government of Texas, the red man and the white man cannot dwell together," he went on to make his meaning plain. "For the present," he said, the Cherokees could

> . . . remain where they are, only because this Government is looking forward to the time, when some peaceable arrangements can be made for their removal, without the necessity of shedding blood, but that their final removal is contemplated, is certain; and that it will be affected, is equally so. Whether it be done by friendly negociation [*sic*] or by the violence of war, must depend upon the Cherokee themselves. If they remain at home quietly and inoffensively, without murdering our people, stealing their property, or giving succor and protection to our enemies, they will be permitted to remain in the undisturbed enjoyment of their present possessions until Congress shall be able to make some final arrangements satisfactory to both parties for their return to their own tribe beyond the Red River. But if listening to the suggestions of bad men equally the enemies of the red man and the white, they shall pursue such a course of conduct as to put in jeopardy the lives and property of our citizens, or to destroy that sense of security essential to the

> happiness and prosperity of our frontier, the inevitable consequence will be a prompt and sanguinary war, which can terminate only in their destruction or expulsion.[16]

At the end of the reading, Duwali was silent. Then, declining to make an immediate response, he protested that he must first "consult his chiefs and headmen." Promising an answer within ten days, he immediately called a council.[17] Debate must have been acrimonious, with Duwali counseling patience and younger men arguing for war against the Texans. Around the first of June the Texas emissaries returned to Duwali's village to receive his reply.[18]

The aged chief explained that he and Gatunwali had been unable to persuade the people to reach a consensus for peace. Resigned to moving, Duwali told Lacy and Reagan that he and John Ross, principal chief of the Eastern Cherokees, had been corresponding for years on the possibility of moving the Cherokees to California. While he did not say that California would be their destination after leaving Texas, he asked for enough time for his followers to raise and harvest the year's crops.[19] Duwali's request was denied. On June 27 Lamar appointed Vice President David G. Burnet, Secretary of War Albert Sidney Johnston, General Thomas J. Rusk, Isaac W. Burton, and James S. Mayfield as commissioners to effect the "immediate removal of the Cherokee Indians, and the ultimate removal of all other emigrant tribes now residing in Texas. . . ."[20]

Shortly thereafter, Rusk led his regiment into the field, camping on a creek a few miles south of Duwali's village. There the general and the other commissioners opened negotiations with the Indians. On July 9 Rusk notified Duwali that a presidential commission had been appointed "to arrange for the removal of the Cherokees from the Territory of Texas."[21] He also informed the chief that his people would be paid for their improvements and for the corn left behind. Finally, he invited the immigrant chiefs to come to the Texas camp and talk.[22] The general's message was delivered to Duwali by Colonel Hugh McLeod and several other officers. They approached the Cherokee village warily, under a white flag, as

Duwali had sent word that he would consider any large group to be a hostile party. After a few minutes' discussion, the chief agreed to come to Camp Johnston, where the Texans were camped on "Council Creek," on July 10.[23]

On that day, Duwali, in the company of twenty-one Indians, including Shawnee chief Spy Buck, met the delegates. The Cherokee representatives refused to talk until Gatunwali could be summoned. On July 11 they gathered briefly and were joined by Delaware chief Harris. In this meeting General Rusk did most of the talking, reminding Duwali that "I once marched 700 men through your nation [and] done you no damage. We do not wish to injure you now unless you force us to do it." He added that if the Cherokees persisted in being "friendly with the wild Indians and Mexicans, we will be forced to kill your people in defence of our frontier. You are between two fires [and] if you remain you will be destroyed."[24] There was no mistaking the officer's intent, and Duwali answered by saying that he "had not much to say today" but would have more to say the next day, when Gatunwali would be present. Once again the negotiations were delayed by Gatunwali's absence; the Cherokees may have been playing for time, perhaps in order to muster their fighting force or to effect the dispersal of women and children from the villages to places of safety.

During the course of the meeting on July 12, Duwali made a lengthy speech. Prefacing his remarks by stating that he believed his decision "would be sanctioned" by the rest of his people, he agreed to "part in peace and friendship. I will return the road we came and go to my people whence we came." But he added that the young men could not leave immediately but would "go as soon as they can get supplies. They have no ammunition to kill game, [and] some delay will be necessary to get provisions."[25] Spy Buck, representing Chief Linney of the Shawnees, spoke next and said that his people would need two months to prepare for the move. Rusk then adjourned the meeting, and all agreed to resume their discussion in two days.

On July 14 Duwali and twenty other Indians came to Council Creek for a final meeting with Rusk, Johnston, Burnet, Burton, and Mayfield. At the beginning of the meeting, Rusk spread blankets on the ground, in traditional Cherokee fashion, and invited the chiefs to sit. Signalling that he was generally hostile to the proceedings, Duwali said that he preferred to sit on the bare earth, and Key, another chief, agreed. Rusk eventually persuaded Duwali to sit on the blankets, but Key was adamant, taking a seat on the ground. After these awkward preliminaries, the commissioners recited their plan for the Indians' departure.[26]

The plan of "removal . . . from the territory and people of Texas" was brief. The Cherokees and their associated bands, the Delawares and Shawnees, were to leave in peace, and the Texas government would pay them "just compensation" for their improvements, crops, and property. Appraisers were to be appointed by President Lamar, subject to Duwali's approval, and payment would be made in goods and in cash. Texas promised to provide supplies to destitute families, and to pay the cash amount when the Cherokees reached U.S. territory. Texas troops would escort the Indians to protect them from the "wild Indians." Finally, "as a guarantee that the Cherokees and others will act in good faith," the Indians were to remove the locks from their guns and leave these items with the military escort until the Indians reached the United States.[27]

Duwali immediately objected to these terms. His first complaint concerned the military escort; he said that he "had come into this country by himself and wished to return in the same way."[28] Concerning the gunlocks, he noted that this particular requirement "ought to have been stated to him before" and that his men were sure to object strenuously to it.[29] In response, the commissioners stated frankly that they did not trust the Cherokees as long as they were armed, because the Indians were suspected of being in collusion with the Mexicans. Apparently offended, Duwali refused to sign the agreement, because his people would object to it (although he added that the business of gunlocks "makes no difference for we have no ammunition").[30] He agreed to call a council to present the articles to the other chiefs, promising to deliver their answer to Mayfield the next morning.

On July 15 Colonel Mayfield and several other officers set

out to obtain Duwali's signature on the plan. The chief said he might be willing to talk, but stated he "had much trouble with his young men, that their minds were much disturbed," and he could not persuade them to agree.[31] He added that many of his followers had already left the country, and for his part, he would call Gatunwali, Harris, and "all the old men" and tell them that he was also going to leave. Pressed by Mayfield to sign the "terms of removal," Duwali replied that it was better to bring all of the chiefs together, because those who were not present "might not agree to it and that it would make a difference."[32] Nonetheless, the commissioners insisted that he sign for Harris and Gatunwali.

Therefore, Duwali "told some six or eight who were sitting and standing around, to go to their council house and talk upon what they had heard. Seven or eight of the elder looking Indians withdrew and seated themselves under a shed close by. . . ."[33] After lengthy deliberations, the council refused to let the chief sign. They directed him to send for Gatunwali and Harris and told him to tell the commissioners to return in three days. When Mayfield pointed out that the army was scheduled to take the field that day in pursuit of the "wild" Indians, and that the chief would have to go to the commissioners' camp and arrange for the delay, Duwali dictated a note to the delegates and sent it with one of his men.[34] In this message the chief explained that "there are but few of us here and cannot go into this arrangement without Chief Big Mush and Harris join it. If so, there will be no further difficulty. I will send for them today and will meet you the day after tomorrow at the same place. It will be best for them all to be together, when the gun locks are taken off."[35]

Mayfield dutifully transmitted the message, which was not well received by the commissioners. Determining from Duwali's actions that the chief was stalling and that "no friendly arrangement could be made . . . ," they sent a message informing him that the army was on its way to his camp and that if the Indians "manifested hostilities," they would be attacked.[36] If, however, they decided to sign the agreement, they were to raise a white flag and give up their guns. When Mayfield and the other officers returned with the message, the village was empty, for the Indians had decamped. Pursued by Texans under the command of Gen. Kelsey H. Douglass, the Cherokees took the initiative and "raised the war whoop and fired" upon their enemies.[37] At dusk on July 15, the first battle was briefly joined a few miles north of Duwali's village. Eighteen Indians died; two Texans were killed. When night fell, the fighting stopped, and the Texans gathered up a store of supplies—lead, powder, and provisions—abandoned by Duwali's forces.[38]

The Cherokees and their allies began moving northward before the sun rose on the sixteenth. They retreated up the Neches River, stopping near its headwaters in present Van Zandt County. The exact number of Cherokees in this encampment is unknown, although an estimated five hundred warriors are supposed to have taken part in the next day's battle. To muster such a large force, Duwali called upon Gatunwali's people as well as Delawares, Shawnees, and Kickapoos. The warriors took up a defensive position in the river bottom. On July 16 Burleson and Rusk, moving north with a force of 250 men, passed through and burned the Delaware village and met the Cherokees, Delawares, Shawnees, and Kickapoos in battle. Despite Duwali's assertion that his men were short of arms and ammunition, they were able to repulse two charges before they were overrun.[39]

At the end, Duwali stood wounded and virtually alone on the field of battle. The eighty-three-year-old chief met death that day, shot in the head at close range by a Texas militiamen. Gatunwali also died, along with one hundred others. At dusk the survivors returned to recover the bodies of the wounded and the slain; even the hard-bitten Rusk was moved to remark that "from the trails of blood, . . . they must have suffered severely."[40] On the morning of July 17 no Indians remained to renew the fight. Defeated and demoralized, the Cherokees and their allied forces splintered into small groups and wandered for weeks without provisions.

A few returned to their east Texas homes, only to find their cabins razed and their fields trampled.[41] Only one Cherokee, Dempsey Fields, nephew of the late chief Richard Fields, received the promised compensation for crops and cattle.[42] One large party returned to the forks of the Trinity, to the vicinity of their original Texas settlement, where they made a temporary encampment on the east fork.[43] In the spring of 1840 some may have joined with Caddoes, Shawnees, and Delawares on the upper Brazos River in making temporary villages and planting crops.[44]

Others joined with Mexican forces on the frontier. In August General Manuel Arista, based in Matamoros, heard rumors that Cherokees and other tribes were massing at the headwaters of the Brazos. He sent them a message promising arms and ammunition to assist in the recovery of "their" land.[45] Some may have responded to the general's offer; soon, Cherokees went southward, joining forces with Vicente Cordova, who was ranging between San Antonio and Matamoros. Eighty Cherokee warriors were reportedly traveling with the Mexican agent in early 1840.[46]

Still others of the displaced hastened across the Red River into the southeastern portion of Indian Territory. Perhaps as many as fifteen hundred settled here and there in the Choctaw reserve. But the Choctaws objected to sharing their territory, and the Cherokees were prompted to move again. They congregated between the Canadian and Washita rivers (south of present-day Norman and west of present-day Ada, Oklahoma).[47] In the spring of 1840, a large number moved to a point near Tahchee's settlement, at the confluence of the Canadian and Arkansas rivers.[48]

The Texas Cherokees who were voluntarily rejoining the nation in Indian Territory in 1839 and 1840 were ill equipped to deal with the level of acculturation of their kinsmen. The newcomers seem to have been virtually ignored by their fellow citizens, which may well indicate that the Texas Indians could make no claim to social, political, or economic standing. Perhaps because of their inadequate acculturation the Western Cherokees may have considered them too inexperienced for political service. None appears to have assumed a political role or to have taken up offices. The situation was probably conditioned by two factors. First, as the Texas Cherokees were destitute, they probably settled on the fringes of the populated areas so that they could find room to hunt and plant in the proper seasons. Second, the nation was in an unstable condition in 1839 and 1840, with political unrest and violence complicating a period of adjustment as three divergent groups were thrown together on the nation's land in Indian Territory.

In 1839 formerly separate parts of the Cherokee nation were reunited, physically if not in spirit, in Indian Territory—present-day Oklahoma. Reunion brought together segments that had parted in the early 1800s, when one group moved across the Mississippi River to become the Western Cherokee nation (with an offshoot becoming the Texas Cherokees) and the other remained in the East as the Eastern Cherokee nation. During the decades between 1800 and 1839 each had followed its own course of development. Accommodation and acculturation, followed by a nationalistic revival, had rapidly changed the character of Eastern Cherokee society, economy, and government.[49] The Western Cherokees changed their customs and mode of living more slowly than did their eastern kinsmen, but they too restricted some social practices and created a governmental system resembling that in the East.[50] In the early and mid-1830s, however, Eastern Cherokee emigrants coming into the western nation brought with them ideas and attitudes new to the Westerners, or Old Settlers, setting the stage for future change and future conflicts.

Even more traditional were the Western Cherokees who lived in Texas; their lifeways in 1839 resembled more the culture of the Principal People at the turn of the century than that of acculturated Cherokees in 1839. The Texas Cherokees still practiced shifting riverine agriculture, lived in towns, had a limited government with clearly defined peace and war chiefs and councillors, and still retained practices of clan revenge involving warfare with their neighbors. While they had taken up many material things from European culture, they were reluctant to adopt ideas and attitudes. And in Texas, because they lived on the frontier, they were unable to obtain material goods that had been readily available in the East and were fairly accessible in Arkansas. Concomitantly, intermarriage with Europeans and Americans had exposed Eastern Cherokees to cultural concepts that were practical and adaptable to

Cherokee life. In Texas, however, contact with whites had been limited to a few diplomatic relationships. Isolated from the body of the Western Cherokee nation, and far removed geographically and ideationally from the Eastern Cherokee nation, the Texas Cherokees must have been viewed as a cultural anomaly when they rejoined the western nation in 1839.

During the 1820s and 1830s the Cherokees who had settled on the Arkansas and Canadian rivers and along both sides of the Neosho and Illinois rivers had experienced transitions in their lifeways. Contemporary observers provided an overview of the Western Cherokees' life-style in this period. They no longer lived in towns, but their farmsteads were scattered across the country. Land was held in common, and no individual landownership was allowed. Their fields were tended "after the fashion of the whites," by intensive cultivation. Hunting had taken second place to agriculture. Beef, butter, and corn were produced in sufficient quantity to support a regional market. But mills were lacking, and corn was ground by pounding. Their houses were both log cabins and frame houses with plank floors, shingled roofs, and stone chimneys. Many owned slaves. The younger men wore European clothing, while a few, primarily the elderly men, still wore turbans, tunics, leggings, and moccasins. The women dressed in European fashions.[51]

Despite the acculturated nature of subsistence and attire, evidence of traditional social forms persisted in the late 1830s. As with the Texas Cherokees, traditional ceremonies were practiced. Seven distinct clans were still recognized, and one observer noted that, "by one of the established rules of the nation, persons of the same clan are prohibited from marrying with each other. . . ." Children were still counted in the mother's lineage. Polygyny, a practice long since outlawed in the eastern nation, was still practiced by a few men in the West.[52]

Changes, however, were apparent, and these set the Cherokees of Arkansas apart from the Texas Cherokees. Educational practices similar to those in the East were present in the western nation. Three missionary schools had been established, and in these the Cherokee syllabary was taught, although fewer than one hundred scholars attended. Nonetheless, more than half of the nation were able to read and write in the Cherokee script. Only a few, however, adhered to the Christian denominations and attended the mission churches.[53]

The political system of the Cherokees in Arkansas was much more elaborate than that of the Texas Cherokees. A national government, which the Western Cherokees had created in the 1820s, consisted of three principal chiefs and two legislative houses. The first, called the Committee, consisted of two representatives from each of four districts; the second, called the Council, also consisted of two representatives from each of four districts. This legislative and executive system was described by American observers as being patterned after the republican form prevalent in the United States. Nevertheless, consensus remained the ruling principle.[54] The judicial system was an innovation with roots in another world. Each of the nation's four districts had a judicial mechanism, in the form of courts, and an enforcement mechanism, in the form of sheriffs.[55] While it sufficed for the needs of the people in the West, the governmental system of the Western Cherokees was much simpler than that of the eastern nation with its constitutional base and elaborate mechanisms for making and enforcing and adjudicating law.

Development of the Western Cherokee nation was complicated by a move to the West in the early 1830s. In May 1828 in a treaty with the United States, the western nation had agreed to give up the reservation in Arkansas and take up 7 million acres further west, in the northeastern corner of present-day Oklahoma.[56] Despite some opposition to the treaty, the Western Cherokees moved westward again. By 1839 the Old Settlers were firmly established in new homes, their population numbering six thousand.[57]

The year 1839 was a desperate one for Cherokees, Western and Eastern alike. Removal of the Cherokee nation from Georgia began in the summer of 1838, superintended by John Ross, General Winfield S. Scott, and seven thousand United States troops. Then came the time of the Trail of Tears, as eighteen thousand Cherokees left their houses and most of their possessions and traveled many hard miles to Indian Territory. Thousands died along the way. Those who survived, called "Emigrants," met a cold welcome from the Old Settlers.[58] And it was in the summer of 1839 that the Cherokees of Texas were forced by the Republic of Texas to leave their homes and move into the Indian Territory. The Western Cherokees, already in Indian Territory, were hard pressed to accommodate the influx of thousands of virtually destitute Emigrant Cherokee families. Not surprisingly, factional strife intensified, resulting in a period of lawlessness. Reincorporation of three peoples into one would take years and would be a difficult experience for the nation.

Tahchee, who had returned to U.S. territory in 1831 and had become one of the three principal chiefs of the Western Cherokees, pled the Texas fugitives' case to General Matthew Arbuckle, in command of U.S. forces at Fort Gibson, near the chief's village. In May 1840 the chief took one of the Texas Cherokees, no doubt a diplomat and perhaps Duwali's or Gatunwali's successor, to see the general. The two explained that the Texas contingent now numbered 180 at Tahchee's village, with many others camped on the Arkansas River at the mouth of the Canadian and more arriving every day. Having no food to give them, the chief appealed to Arbuckle to furnish provisions. Somewhat reluctantly, the general did so, but he immediately wrote to the Emigrants' council and asked them to provide rations for three or four months.[59] The council replied that "under the existing circumstances" its members were "at a loss to make any reply whatsoever."[60] Later, Arbuckle complained to the council that Sequoyah (George Guess), an Old Settler, had "urged them [the Texas Cherokees] not to return to their nation," and that because of his advice, many of them were not going to join the Cherokees on the reservation.[61] Apparently, neither the Old Settlers nor the Emigrant Cherokees welcomed the return of the Texas Cherokees to the fold.

Throughout late 1839 and in 1840 some of the Texas Cherokees carried on a war of retribution against Texas, using the nation's reservation as a base of operations. They approached Tahchee and asked for his participation, but he refused.[62]

Throughout 1840 these disgruntled and homeless ones picked away at settlements in Texas. Unrest along the U.S.-Texas border caused considerable consternation among American and Cherokee officials alike. With the arrival of Texas Cherokees among the Choctaws, U.S. military officials were prompted to predict that men from all of the displaced southeastern tribes might rally to the Cherokees in a war against Texas.[63] In late August the Republic of Texas sent a ranger company to scout the Red River area for Cherokees who might be crossing back and forth, but none were encountered.[64] The U.S., Texas, and Cherokee governments eventually cooperated in transporting of few captured Cherokees north to Indian Territory. In April 1840 the Cherokee council requested General Arbuckle to pursue the extradition of any Cherokees who might be held prisoner in Texas. Arbuckle and Branch T. Archer, Texas secretary of war, subsequently arranged for the transportation of twelve men, women, and children to Fort Jesup, Louisiana.[65] So desperate were American officials to prevent an international war that Arbuckle finally begged the Cherokee council to try to prevent further hostilities by Cherokees under their jurisdiction.[66]

At this time, there were still many of the nation living a fugitive existence in Texas, and others had taken up residence in Mexico. In 1840 and 1841 Cherokees were maintaining encampments on the upper Brazos.[67] In 1840 a scouting party of Cherokees led by John Brown traveled from Indian Territory to Monclova and petitioned Mexican officials to give them land where they could farm and raise stock. It is reasonable to suggest that the guides may have been Texas Cherokees. The government of Mexico denied them permission to settle until they could provide precise information on the number who would relocate.[68] Nonetheless, a few did move to Mexico. In the spring of 1842 Sequoyah went in search of these Cherokees, and he found them living in San Fernando, on the lower Rio Grande, in the state of Coahuila.[69]

In Texas, Cherokees continued to fight alongside Mexican troops. In the summer of 1842, when a Mexican force under General Adrian Woll invaded Texas and captured San Antonio, Cherokees saw action in the battle of Salado Creek, six miles east of the town. Cherokee agent Vicente Cordova met his death in the battle, as did ten or eleven of the Cherokees.[70] Disastrous for the Mexicans, this fiasco convinced Woll to withdraw across the Rio Grande. The encounter, coupled with Sam Houston's reemergence as a political force, may have influenced the Cherokees to abandon the Mexican cause at last.

When Sam Houston, the Cherokees' adopted kinsman, was elected to a second presidential term late in 1841, he immediately inaugurated an Indian policy calculated to forestall future hostilities with immigrant nations. During 1842 and 1843 he sent commissioners to make treaties with all of the indigenous Indians and the remaining immigrant Indians. On September 29, 1843, representatives of the Cherokees, led by "Captain" Chicken Trotter, as well as chiefs of the Delawares, Chickasaws, Caddoes, Tawakonis, Kichais, Biloxis, and Wacos, signed a treaty of friendship with the republic at Bird's Fort, on the Trinity River.[71] Subsequently, Cherokees received goods from the republic's government.[72] A similar treaty was concluded on October 9, 1844, between commissioners of the republic and leaders of the Cherokees, Delawares, Shawnees, Tawakonis, Lipans, Ionis, Anadarkos, Caddoes, Kichais, and Comanches. This second treaty provided for an annual council of these tribes to be held at Tawakoni Creek (near present-day Waco).[73] On September 12, 1845, the commissioners reconvened on this site for a council, which was attended by representatives of the Cherokees, Anadarkos, Caddoes, Delawares, Ionis, Lipans, and Tonkawas (although these last were not included in the 1844 treaty).[74] Among the Cherokee representatives could have been some of those known to be residing on the Red River, including Duwali's son, Standing Bowls, or those residing on the Brazos, including Sequoyah's son.[75]

Soon after this council, a delegation of fifty-four Western Cherokees, or Old Settlers, arrived in Texas looking for a home. On August 31 they left Evansville, Arkansas, where they had fled during a period of internecine violence in the early 1840s.[76] The explorers reached the Trinity River in mid-September 1845, and on October 11 they came upon a Cherokee village near the confluence of the Bosque River with the Brazos River, near present-day Waco. Some of the Cherokees living here had recently returned from a period of residence in Mexico. After this, the exploring party went out onto the prairie and then returned to Arkansas.[77] As a result of this mission, the Old Settlers soon petitioned the U.S. goverment to give them permission to move to Texas.[78]

But an anticipated separation was not to become reality. A U.S. commission investigating affairs in the Cherokee nation decided that union was more viable than separation. In late summer 1846 representatives of all Cherokee factions met in the U.S. capital, where on August 6 their leaders signed an agreement specifying that the lands in the nation were for common use.[79] With all factions represented at the signing of the treaty it appeared that at last the Cherokee nation was officially united, in law if not yet in spirit.

As a cultural unit the Cherokees always experienced a dichotomy between the cultural ideal of harmony and the social reality of division. To maintain harmony, interpersonal relations had always been guided by the concept of self-effacement. Concomitantly, politics had always been guided by the concept that consensus and cooperation is necessary to any action—for organizing work, production, and ceremony as well as for practicing diplomacy and pursuing war. But harmonious interaction of Cherokees as human beings was limited by the needs of individuals and groups, most particularly, clans. Individuals who disagreed with group consensus were not prohibited from pursuing an independent course, especially in clan affairs or in military affairs. Indeed, the pursuit of clan revenge might often countermand a consensus for peace reached by a village or a national council.

In Cherokee social organization, factionalism was institutionalized as part of the political process. It served as a safety valve, as an acceptable way of dealing with divergent opinions and the necessities of clan obligations. In nonthreatening circumstances, before the arrival of Europeans, when the Cherokees were dealing only with other Indian societies, it worked passably well. After the arrival of Europeans, however, factionalism complicated many delicate diplomatic situations. As Cherokee leaders negotiated with Europeans and then with Americans for peace and for land cessions, the Indians' tendency toward political polarization was accentuated. It was dangerous for Cherokee factions to contradict a village, regional, or national consensus for war or peace, but, consistently, they did so. In the era of wars and treaties, between 1721 and 1794, militant, anti-land-cession factions repeatedly warred first against Europeans and then against the United States, bringing about serious consequences for all of the people. This context recurred repeatedly in every region inhabited by the Cherokees and in every historical period for which there are records. Clan revenge and factional disputes resulting from the "opting out" rule played havoc with Cherokee diplomacy in the American South, in Arkansas, and in Texas.

Factionalism was the operative cultural practice that prevailed to maintain a tripartite Cherokee nation for nearly half a century. The southeastern tribes in general were open to change, willing to adapt and adopt and move whenever necessary to make life more tolerable for groups of like-minded individuals. When Cherokees in the late eighteenth century decided that they could not live with current social and political developments in the nation, they moved westward across the Mississippi into new lands. By this process the Western Cherokee nation was created before the turn of the nineteenth century, by this process the Western Cherokees came to find homes in Texas in the third decade of that century, and by this process Western Cherokees came back to Texas seeking a refuge in 1845.

Underlying this divergence in the development of the three portions of the nation, however, was the persistence of tradition. Grace Woodward, in her history of the Cherokees, notes (somewhat ethnocentrically):

> Between 1841–1846, certain members of the tribe reverted to the barbarism of the ancients. When a member of a family or clan met death at the hands of an enemy, the latter was finished off by relatives of the deceased before he could be brought to trial. Thirty-three such murders were reported over a period of nine months in the Cherokee Nation, and drunken-

> ness increased accordingly. Despite the efforts made by law-abiding Cherokees to curb this disorder, crime appeared to flourish on controversy and disunion, a disunion which perilously verged on civil war.[80]

For untold centuries the rules of clan membership had been the strongest of all concepts organizing Cherokee society. Clan revenge had been abolished by both Eastern and Western Cherokees in the early 1800s, but nonetheless, among the Western Cherokees and Texas Cherokees it continued to be the primary operative principle in Cherokees' relations with their neighbors. Even after the union of the tribe in the mid-1840s, Emigrants, Old Settlers, and Texas Cherokees continued to have their factional differences, and they once again became involved in the pursuit of vengeance. What its recurrence at this point may mean is not that Cherokees "reverted to the barbarism of the ancients," but that new rules had lost their viability in the present situation, while old rules, presumably buried by acculturated forms of behavior, became once again meaningful as a way of dealing with present circumstances. No matter how unacceptable to those holding more acculturated attitudes, tradition had been persistent. No matter how acculturated they may appear to have been, no matter how westernized their appearance, Cherokees were Cherokees. The ambience of their culture was and will be always reflected in ideas and social practices typically Cherokee. The hopes for cultural unity so graphically presented in the agreement of 1846 between Old Settlers and Emgirants was overly optimistic. In the future, the Principal People would continue to face intracultural conflict so functional in Cherokee society and so characteristic of Cherokee politics that it was destined to remain forever a part of Cherokee life.

Epilogue

*There is change indeed in dress and seeming, but the heart of the Indian is still his own.—James Mooney (*Myths of the Cherokees, *12).*

Texas continued to beckon to Cherokees as the Civil War began. In the years before the war, the nation once again divided ranks over the question of neutrality. John Ross, chief officer of the Cherokee nation, opposed alignment with either Union or Confederacy, but Stand Watie led a "Southern Rights Party" determined to fight for the South. The Confederacy gave Watie guns and ammunition and offered a half-million dollars for the Cherokee Neutral Land, a twenty-five-mile strip extending fifty miles north of the Cherokees' reservation. In late 1861 Ross, fearing Confederate invasion, allied the nation with the South. War raged in Indian Territory, but by 1863 Union loyalists and Union troops were slowly defeating the Confederate Cherokees.[1]

Many of the Southern partisans' families fled to the Red River, and of these, many pushed further south into Texas. Among the refugees was the wife of Stand Watie, who took up residence with her sister and brother-in-law, Nancy and George Starr, who had come to Texas at least as early as 1850.[2] Other Cherokees settled near Tyler, Kilgore, Mount Pleasant, and Waco. By the end of the war there may have been as many as one hundred families of "Southern" Cherokees in Texas.[3] Most returned to Indian Territory in 1865 and 1866, their citizenship in the nation restored by an act of the national government in October 1866.[4]

From the 1840s through the midtwentieth century, the Principal People pursued compensation for Texas lands lost in 1839. In the mid-1850s the nation sent William P. Adair to Washington, D.C., to petition Congress for permission to sue the state of Texas for the return of 1.5 million acres in east Texas. Texas offered to compensate the Cherokees with 14 million acres in the Texas Panhandle; the nation declined.[5]

After the end of the Civil War, Adair continued to prosecute the nation's claim. At some point in the process, he formed a thirteen-share partnership to raise capital to reactivate the suit. Among the partners were Judge Richard Fields, a descendant of Texas chief Richard Fields, and C. N. Vann, a descendant of Andrew Vann. In 1871 Adair and Vann, representing the "successors of the Texas Cherokees," contracted with John C. Frémont and J. Eliott Condict to negotiate the sale of land recovered in the suit, should it be successful. Frémont was to receive one-fourth of the proceeds of all sales. This effort, too, failed, although in 1882–1883 an attempt was made to revive the suit, using evidence earlier compiled by Adair and Vann.[6]

In 1915, nine hundred "heirs of Texas Cherokees" hired George Fields, an attorney, to represent them in a $100 million lawsuit against the state of Texas. The claimants sought compensation for the loss of lands nearly one century before. In 1920 Fields instituted a petition with the U.S. Supreme Court, asking permission to sue, but the petition was denied.[7] In 1924 John Taylor, attorney for the claimants, attempted to enlist the commissioner of Indian affairs in their cause, to no avail.[8] In 1948 the Cherokees filed a claim against the U.S. government, asking for $5 million in compensation. The case was heard before the Indian Claims Commission, which denied the suit's validity.[9]

Finally, and most recently, in 1963, Earl Boyd Pearce, general counsel for the Cherokees, petitioned the State of Texas for redress of grievances nearly 125 years old. Pearce's plan was ingenious: he proposed that the Cherokees' claim be examined by a committee of historians, and when its legitimacy had been established, compensation would be made by means of free education for one thousand Cherokees of half-blood or greater over a twenty-five year period in state-supported universities in Texas. The funding for this would come from a cash settlement of one dollar per acre, to be held in trust by the state of Texas. In an opinion delivered in March 1964, Texas's Attorney General Waggoner Carr denied the validity of any Cherokee claim against the state of Texas, which, he said, was no longer liable for claims against the Republic of Texas.[10]

Two centuries have passed since Cherokees first crossed the Mississippi River and ventured westward to make new homes in strange lands. It is now a century and a half since the Texas Cherokees were pushed from their homes and farms and rejoined their kinsmen in Indian Territory. Cherokees today still bear the surnames of headmen and ordinary Indians whose family stories survive in Texas history. They have long memories, and the descendants of Texas Cherokees will not soon forget this important part of their past.

Notes

Abbreviations

AJHP	Andrew Jackson Houston Papers
ATEC	Appendix to Translations of Empresario Contracts
BA	Bexar Archives
BAE	Bureau of American Ethnology
LROSW	Letters Received in the Office of the Secretary of War
NA	Nacogdoches Archives
RCAT	Records of the Cherokee Agency in Tennessee
RTEC	Records of Translations of Empresario Contracts
THSC	Texas Historical Survey Committee

1. The Cherokees Come to Texas

1. James G. Mooney, *Myths of the Cherokees, Nineteenth Annual Report of the Bureau of American Ethnology, 1897–1898,* 391.
2. Ibid.; Robert H. Lowie, *Indians of the Plains,* 72–77; W. W. Newcomb, Jr., *The Indians of Texas,* 63–64, 77–78, 150–52, 310–20, 327.
3. Mooney, *Myths,* 17; David Corkran, "Cherokee Pre-History," *North Carolina Historical Review* 34 (1957), 456–57; William H. Gilbert, Jr., *The Eastern Cherokees,* Bulletin 133, Bureau of American Ethnology (hereafter cited as BAE), 314.
4. Mooney, *Myths,* 20.
5. John E. Swanton, *Indians of the Southeastern United States,* Bulletin

137, BAE, 114; Roy S. Dickens, Jr., "The Origins and Development of Cherokee Culture," in *The Cherokee Indian Nation: A Troubled History,* ed. Duane H. King, 10; Malone, *Cherokees of the Old South,* 3.

6. Dickens, "Origins," 12–13; Roy S. Dickens, *Cherokee Prehistory: The Pisgah Phase in the Appalachian Summit Region,* 13–15, 213–14; Frank M. Setzler and Jesse D. Jennings, "Peachtree Mound and Village Site, Cherokee County, North Carolina," Bulletin 135, BAE, 55–57.

7. While the present study is limited to the history and ethnography of Cherokees who lived in Texas, many interpretations were necessarily drawn from studies of specific aspects of Cherokee life and politics in the eighteenth and early nineteenth centuries; references to these works are made when warranted. Interested readers are invited to consult the following works for an overview of Cherokee history and culture. There exists no published ethnographic overview of putative pre-Columbian Cherokee culture, but for a general treatment of the southeastern culture area, see Charles M. Hudson, *The Southeastern Indians,* and John E. Swanton, *Indians of the Southeastern United States,* Bulletin 137, BAE.

For analysis of archeological evidence of pre-Columbian Cherokee culture, see Dickens, *Cherokee Pre-History;* Dickens's article, "The Origins and Development of Cherokee Culture," in *The Cherokee Nation: A Troubled History,* ed. Duane H. King; Frank M. Setzler and Jesse D. Jennings, "Peachtree Mound and Village Site, Cherokee County, North Carolina," Bulletin 135, BAE; and William S. Webb, *An Archeological Survey of the Norris Basin in Eastern Tennessee,* Bulletin 118, BAE.

A considerable number of works provide insight into specific aspects of Cherokee society in the early decades of Cherokee-white contact; the reader should consult Leonard Bloom, "The Cherokee Clan: A Study in Acculturation," *American Anthropologist* 41 (1939); Raymond D. Fogelson and Paul Kutsche, "Cherokee Economic Cooperatives: The Gadugh," Bulletin 180, BAE, in *Symposium on Cherokee and Iroquois Culture,* ed. William N. Fenton and John Gulick; Frederick O. Gearing, *Priests and Warriors: Social Structures for Cherokee Politics in the Eighteenth Century,* American Anthropological Association Memoir 93; Gearing, "The Structural Poses of Eighteenth-Century Cherokee Villages," *American Anthropologist* 60 (1958); Gary C. Goodwin, *Cherokees in Transition: A Study in Changing Cultures and Environment Prior to 1775*; Walter B. Miller, "Two Concepts of Authority," *American Anthropologist* 57 (1955); Mooney, *Myths*; Mooney and Franz Olbrechts, *The Summer Manuscript: Cherokee Sacred Formulas and Medicinal Prescriptions,* Bulletin 99, BAE; Theda Perdue, *Slavery and the Evolution of Cherokee Society, 1540–1866;* John Phillip Reid, *A Better Kind of Hatchet: Law, Trade, and Diplomacy in the Cherokee Nation During the Early Years of Contact;* Reid, *A Law of Blood: The Primitive Law of the Cherokee Nation*; and Rennard Strickland, *Fire and the Spirits: Cherokee Law from Clan to Court.*

A general bibliography of works dealing with Cherokee culture, prehistory, and history will be found in Raymond D. Fogelson's *The Cherokees:*

A Critical Bibliography, which contains a useful, if somewhat dated, bibliographical essay.

8. Reid, *A Better Kind of Hatchet*, 2–3; David H. Corkran, *The Cherokee Frontier: Conflict and Survival, 1740–1762*, 3–7; Betty A. Smith, "Distribution of Eighteenth Century Cherokee Settlements," in *The Cherokee Indian Nation: A Troubled History*, ed. King, 48–50; Mooney, *Myths*, 16–17; Corkran, "Pre-History," 461–66. For population estimates of Cherokees at the time of contact, see Mooney, *Myths*, 34; Gearing, *Priests and Warriors*, 31–32; and Charles C. Royce, *The Cherokee Nation of Indians, Fifth Annual Report of the Bureau of American Ethnology, 1883–1884*, 11, 210.

9. Mooney, *Myths*, 202; *The Narrative of the Expedition of Hernando de Soto by the Gentlemen of Elvas*, ed. Theodore H. Lewis, in *Spanish Explorers in the Southern United States, 1528–1543*, ed. Frederick W. Hodge and Theodore H. Lewis, 176–78.

10. Cherokee political and diplomatic history have been the subjects of numerous studies, most of which assume an unfortunately paternalistic, white-oriented viewpoint. While commenting on the rapidity with which the Cherokees acculturated, most of these studies ignore the many causes of change, as well as the processes of change that lay within the structure of Cherokee society. For general political history of the Cherokee nation, interested readers should consult: Mooney, *Myths;* Emmet Starr, *History of the Cherokee Indians and Their Legends and Folklore;* Marion Starkey, *The Cherokee Nation;* and Morris L. Wardell, *A Political History of the Cherokee Nation, 1838–1907.* Other general studies illuminate cultural history and the process of change; these include John R. Finger, *The Eastern Band of Cherokees, 1819–1900;* William H. Gilbert, Jr., *The Eastern Cherokees*, Bulletin 133, BAE; William G. McLoughlin, *Cherokee Renascence in the New Republic* and McLoughlin's *Cherokees and Missionaries, 1789–1839;* Malone, *Cherokees of the Old South;* and Perdue, *Slavery and the Evolution of Cherokee Society.* To place Cherokee acculturation within a theoretical framework, consult the Social Science Research Council's study, "Acculturation: An Exploratory Formulation," *American Anthropologist* 56 (1954).

11. Mooney, *Myths*, 261; Gearing, *Priests and Warriors*, 31–32; William G. McLoughlin, *Cherokees and Missionaries*, 19–23.

12. Gearing, *Priests and Warriors*, 31–32; William N. Fenton, "Factionalism in American Indian Society," *Papers of the Fourth International Congress of Anthropological and Ethnological Science*, 331–40.

13. Gearing, *Priests and Warriors*, 101–3; James P. Pate, "The Chicamauga: A Forgotten Segment of Indian Resistence on the Southern Frontier" (Ph.D. diss., Mississippi State University, 1969); William G. McLoughlin, "Thomas Jefferson and the Beginning of Cherokee Nationalism, 1806–1806," *William and Mary Quarterly* 32 (1975): 547–80. As these works attest, from the mideighteenth century through the first decade of the nineteenth century, factionalism was almost a constant in Cherokee politics and diplomacy, particularly in the debates over land cessions. Factionalism was endemic in Cherokee society as early as the time Europeans

began recording their observations about the tribe's political behavior. Among the historical Cherokees there were always two sides to every question: warriors argued for war, chiefs for peace; the old argued for tradition, the young for change; region vied with region for dominance in tribal council meetings and over signing or rejecting treaties. It is possible that over the centuries new settlement areas and even new regions were created as much by dissenters withdrawing and relocating as by groups "hiving off" for ecological reasons.

14. Treaty of Holston, 1791, in Charles J. Kappler, comp., *Indian Affairs: Laws and Treaties* 2:29–32.

15. Changes in Cherokee culture after 1791 are chronicled in Malone, *Cherokees of the Old South,* 74–83, and are amplified in Woodward, *The Cherokees*, 120–26, 140–46, 154–56. A number of studies deal with changes in specific cultural traits; see Leonard Bloom, "The Acculturation of the Eastern Cherokees: Historical Aspects," *North Carolina Historical Review* 19 (1942): 349–51; and Gilbert, *The Eastern Cherokees,* 361. William G. McLoughlin's two recent works, *Cherokees and Missionaries, 1789–1839* (1984) and *Cherokee Renascence in the New Republic* (1986) outline in great detail the changes and continuities in the Cherokees' world view and spiritual life in the pre-removal period.

16. McLoughlin, *Cherokee Renascence,* 145–65; Mooney, *Myths,* 82–83.

17. Letter of Colonel Morgan, to Mssrs. Turnbull and Co., Ft. Pitt, 14 April 1789, in Louis Houck, ed., *The Spanish Regime in Missouri: A Collection of Papers and Documents Relating to Upper Louisiana* 1:280–81.

18. Alvarez to Perez, 10 May 1788, in Laurence Kinnaird, ed., *Spain in the Mississippi Valley, 1765–1794, Translations of Materials from the Spanish Archives in the Bancroft Library, Annual Report of the American Historical Association for the Year 1945,* 2:254–55.

19. Perez to Miró, 31 May 1788, in Kinnaird, ed., *Spain in the Mississippi Valley* 2:255; Miró to Robertson, 20 April 1789, ibid., 2:268–69.

20. Letter of Colonel Morgan, 14 April 1789, in Houck, ed., *Spanish Regime* 1:280–81; Mattie Austin Hatcher, "The Louisiana Background of the Colonization of Texas, 1763–1803," *Southwestern Historical Quarterly* 24 (1921): 30; Morales to Ulloa, 31 March 1797, quoted in Mattie Austin Hatcher, *The Opening of Texas to Foreign Settlement, 1801–1821,* 186–88; Statement of a former Spanish commandant of Arkansas in 1796, by request of Governor William Clark, 5 June 1816, in Clarence E. Carter, ed. and comp., *Territorial Papers of the United States* 15:178–80; Log of His Majesty's Galliot 'La Fleche,' January 5–March 25, 1793, in Kinnaird, ed., *Spain in the Mississippi Valley* 3:127; Journal of Lorimier during the Threatened Genet Invasion of Louisiana, 1793–1795, in Houck, ed., *Spanish Regime* 2:83–85, 98; Kanati to Meigs, 17 June 1811, Records of the Bureau of Indian Affairs, Letters Received, Records of the Cherokee Agency in Tennessee, 1801–1835, Microfilm 208, Roll 5, #2267 (hereafter cited as RCAT, Roll Number, Document Number).

21. "Indian Nations," Nicholas Biddle Notes, *Letters of the Lewis and Clark Expedition, 1783–1854, with Related Documents,* ed. Donald Jackson,

522; *Original Journals of the Lewis and Clark Expedition, 1804–1806,* ed. Reuben Gold Thwaites, 6:112.

22. Meigs to Secretary of War, 22 January 1810, RCAT, Roll 5, #2442; Meigs to Secretary of War, 14 February 1810, RCAT, Roll 5, #2458; Meigs to Governor Blount, 16 February 1810, RCAT, Roll 5, #2461; McLoughlin, *Cherokee Renascence,* 145–59.

23. Passport for 63 Cherokees Moving Over the Mississippi, 10 January 1810, RCAT, Roll 5, #2436; Meigs to Secretary of War, 22 January 1810, RCAT, Roll 5, #2442. See also Smith, "Distribution of Cherokee Settlements," 55–56.

Born circa 1756 of a Scottish father and a full-blood Cherokee mother, Duwali was eminent among the Cherokee chiefs, having been a signer of the Treaty of Holston in 1791. In 1805 he (along with chiefs Doublehead and Talontuskee) signed an unauthorized land cession treaty that proved to be extremely unpopular with the majority of the nation (see Kappler, *Indian Affairs: Laws and Treaties* 2:33 and 2:84, and McLoughlin, *Cherokee Renascence,* 145–59). His emigration in 1810 may be attributable to fear of reprisals by the opposing faction, because disposing of tribal property without unanimous approval of all the clans was punishable by death. This penalty was exacted of Doublehead in 1807.

According to Grant Foreman, *Indians and Pioneers* (1930) and Mary Whatley Clarke, *Chief Bowles and the Texas Cherokees* (1974), the migration of Duwali's people from Tennessee took place in 1794 following an incident of violence, which these two writers attribute to Duwali. Both Foreman and Clarke took their information from the reminiscences of Cephas Washburn, a Presbyterian missionary in Arkansas from 1820 to 1830. Washburn had heard the story in New Orleans from a woman who claimed to be a survivor of the attack. According to her story, Duwali's warriors had attacked a boatload of people led by William and Alexander Scott; the Indians had killed all but the women and children, whom they set adrift. In Washburn's version, repeated by Foreman and Clarke (as well as by several other historians), Duwali and company had run away to Arkansas to avoid punishment. Foreman also referred to a claims adjustment case filed by the Scott family in 1815 (in *American State Papers, Claims,* 1834, 9) and also referred to an article appearing in the *Knoxville Gazette* in September 1794. While both of these sources do relate substantially the same story concerning the incident, neither names Duwali, or "Bowl," as the perpetrator; on the contrary, the *Gazette* article places the leadership of the party with a Cherokee named White-Man-Killer. Emmet Starr, in his *Early History of the Cherokees* (1917) also repeats the error.

Contrary to this bit of folklore, the records indicate that Bowl, or Duwali, emigrated in January 1810. He is specifically named in travel documents issued to him by the U.S. agent for the Cherokees, R. J. Meigs. The Indians were "looking for good hunting grounds" west of the Mississippi. They were residents of a town located 160 miles upstream from the Cherokee agency on the Hiwassee River (Meigs to Secretary of War, 22 Janaury 1810, RCAT, Roll 5, #2442).

A likely explanation for the confusion may lie in Duwali's warlike stance in Arkansas. After Washburn had been in the vicinity of the Arkansas Cherokees for a few months, he would almost certainly have heard a number of stories about Duwali's activities in the Osage war; at this time, the chief was adamantly opposing the consensus for peace with the Osages and was gaining a reputation among Cherokees and American officials as an implacable dissident.

24. Treat to Dearborn, 2 April 1811, Letter Book of the Arkansas Trading House, 171; Meigs to William Eustes, 1 December 1809, RCAT, Roll 4, no document number; see Robert Paul Markman, "The Arkansas Cherokees, 1817–1828" (Ph.D. diss., University of Oklahoma, 1972), for a political history of the Western Cherokees.

25. Talontuskee to Meigs, 23 June 1810, RCAT, Toll 5, #2521; Meigs to Secretary of War, 25 July 1810, RCAT, Roll 5, #2530; Kanati to Meigs, 17 June 1811, RCAT, Roll 5, #2667; McLoughlin, *Cherokee Renascence,* 162–63, 170.

26. Dr. John Sibley, *A Report from Natchitoches in 1807,* ed. Frederick W. Hodge, 16.

27. Swanton, *Indians,* 4; "Names and Probable Numbers of Tribes of Indians within the limits and under the Superintendency of the Natchitoches Agency," 20 November 1816, Records of the Bureau of Indian Affairs, Records of the Secretary of War Relating to Indian Affairs, Letters Received, 1800–1823, Microfilm 271, Roll 1, #0024 (hereafter cited as LROSW with roll number, frame, or document number).

28. Francisco Viana to Antonio Cordéro, 8 August 1807, Bexar Archives (hereafter cited as BA); Antonio Cordéro to Nemesio Salcedo, 4 September 1807, BA; Nemesio Salcedo to Antonio Cordéro, 6 October 1807, BA; Antonio Cordéro to Francisco Viana, 30 October 1807, BA; Salcedo to Cordéro, 6 October 1807, BA.

29. Jane M. Berry, "The Indian Policy of Spain in the Southwest," *Mississippi Valley Historical Review* 3 (1917): 466; Kinnaird, ed., *Spain in the Mississippi Valley* 2:xv; Arthur P. Whitaker, "Spain and the Cherokee Indians, 1793–1798," *North Carolina Historical Review* 4 (1926): 252–60.

30. Henry P. Walker, ed., "William McLane's Narrative of the Magee-Gutiérrez Expedition, 1812–1813," *Southwestern Historical Quarterly* 61 (1963): 578–80.

31. "Names and Probable Numbers," 20 November 1816, LROSW, Roll 1, #0024; Jamison to Secretary of War, 10 May 1817, in Carter, ed., *Territorial Papers* 15:302.

32. Jedidiah Morse, *A Report to the Secretary of War of the United States on Indian Affairs,* 256–58. In 1812, after a series of earthquakes and floods devastated the St. Francis River region, most of the Cherokees moved high up on the Arkansas River to the foot of the Ozark Mountains. Emmet Starr, in his *History of the Cherokee Indians,* alleges that Duwali's village lay between Shoal and Petit Jean creeks, on the south side of the Arkansas River (p. 187). Thomas Nuttall, the naturalist, visited this place while touring through Arkansas, but he does not mention Duwali in his narrative.

33. The Western Cherokees' reserve lay north of the Arkansas River and

south of the White River. Treaty of 1817, in Kappler, comp., *Indian Affairs* 2:140–44; Register of Cherokees Who Wish to Emigrate to Arkansas River, 8 July 1817, RCAT, Roll 7, #3693; Meigs to Secretary of War, 24 July 1817, RCAT, Roll 7, #3701; John Jolly to Calhoun, 28 January 1818, LROSW, Roll 2, frame #0618; Jolly's Passport, 26 January 1818, RCAT, Roll 7, #3904; Inventory of Stores and Number of Cherokee Emigrants Enrolled for Arkansas, 8 January 1819, RCAT, Roll 8, #4161; Markman, "The Arkansas Cherokees," 83–87, 92–98; McLoughlin, *Cherokee Renascence,* 260.

34. Stephen H. Long to General Thomas A. Smith, 30 January 1818, LROSW, Roll 2, #0835; William Clark to Secretary of War, 30 September 1816, in Carter, ed., *Territorial Papers* 15:177; Secretary of War to Andrew Jackson, 15 December 1818, Records of the Bureau of Indian Affairs, Letters Sent, 1800–1824, Microfilm M15, Roll 4, D:685.

35. "Account of the United States Marshall for the Territory, . . . Returning the fourth census, or enumeration, of the inhabitants of the United States," 2 September 1822, in Carter, ed., *Territorial Papers* 19:458; Henry Conway to Secretary of War, 19 October 1821, in Carter, ed., *Territorial Papers* 19:329.

36. Kappler, ed., *Indian Affairs,* 2:167.

37. Secretary of War to Reuben Lewis, 22 July 1819, in Carter, ed., *Territorial Papers* 19:87–88.

38. Cephas Washburn, *Reminiscences of the Indians,* ed. Rev. J. G. Moore, 113–15; Markman, "The Arkansas Cherokees," 110–12, 131–32; Clark to Secretary of War, 1 July 1818, in Carter, ed., *Territorial Papers* 15:404–5; Clark to Secretary of War, 6 October 1818, 15:454; Lewis to Secretary of War, 16 March 1819, ibid., 19:55–56.

39. Strickland, *Fire and the Spirits,* 27–28; Reid, *A Law of Blood,* 35–48, 73–76, 151–61; Bloom, "The Cherokee Clan: A Study in Acculturation," *American Anthropologist* 41 (1939): 266–68; Hudson, *Southeastern Indians,* 193, 241–44. Among the Cherokees the standard kin group was the clan, a social category whose members reckoned their descent from a common female animal ancestress. In this totemic arrangement, the supposed connection, occurring far back in time, was known only through myth. The Cherokees had seven clans: Wolf, Deer, Bird, Paint, Long Hair, Blue, and Blind Savannah. All clans were represented in each community and performed significant, and occasionally corporate, social, legal, and political functions.

40. *Laws of the Cherokee Nation Adopted by the Council at Various Periods,* 9–10, 19.

41. Washburn, *Reminiscences,* 113–15; Miller to Secretary of War, 20 June 1820, LROSW, Roll 3, Frame 956.

42. Bradford to Secretary of War, 4 March 1820, in Carter, ed., *Territorial Papers* 19:515; Cherokee Council to Reuben Lewis and William Bradford, 10 February 1820, ibid., 19:151–52. Duwali's hatred for the Osages was legendary. He, Takatoka, and Talontuskee had led the Cherokees in the destruction of Osage chief Clermont's village in 1817. In one of the bloodiest military actions ever recorded for this portion of the tribe, the Cherokees set a

trap that took most of the warriors from the town, then burned the village, killed seventy women and children, and took fifty prisoners to hold for ransom (Bradburn to Andrew Jackson, 1 January 1818, Presidential Papers Series, Roll 23). According to witnesses, Bowl (Duwali) struck the first blow.

43. *Arkansas Gazette*, 29 July 1820; Edwin James, *Account of An Expedition from Pittsburgh to the Rocky Mountains, Performed in the Years 1819 and 1820*, ed. Reuben Gold Thwaites, in *Early Western Travels*, 3:22–23; *Laws (1852)*, 85.

44. Thomas Nuttall, *Journal of Travels into the Arkansas Territory, October 2, 1818–February 18, 1820*, ed. Reuben Gold Thwaites, in *Early Western Travels* 13:176.

45. Fowler to McKinney, 14 June 1819, Records of the Bureau of Indian Affairs, Records of the Superintendent of Indian Trade, Letter Book of the Natchitoches-Sulphur Fork Factory, 1809–1821, T1029, frame 73 (hereafter cited as Natchitoches Letter Book; Fowler to McKinney, 2 July 1819, Natchitoches Letter Book, frame 85.

46. Miller to Secretary of War, 28 May 1820, in *Arkansas Gazette*, 15 July 1820; Miller to Secretary of War, 20 June 1820, LROSW, Roll 3, frame 956; John H. Reagan, *Memoirs of John Hunter Reagan*, ed. Walter F. McCaleb, 30–31.

47. Morse, *Report*, 373.

48. Map of Texas Compiled from Surveys Recorded in the Land Office of Texas and Other Official Surveys (London: 1841).

49. Sibley, *Report from Natchitoches*, 95; Juan Antonio Padilla, "Report on the Barbarous Indians of the Province of Texas (1819)," trans. M. A. Hatcher, *Southwestern Historical Quarterly* 23 (1919): 47–49.

50. Isaac J. Cox, *Explorations of the Louisiana Frontier, 1803–1805, Annual Report of the American Historical Association for the Year 1904*, 158; Rex W. Strickland, "Miller County, Arkansas Territory, the Frontier that Men Forgot," *Chronicles of Oklahoma* 28 (1940): 17.

51. Sibley to Secretary of War, 7 July 1811, in Julia K. Garrett, ed. and comp., "Doctor John Sibley and the Louisiana-Texas Frontier, 1803–1814, *Southwestern Historical Quarterly* 49 (1945): 119.

52. Jamison to Secretary of War, 31 March 1817, in Carter, ed., *Territorial Papers* 15:257; David Music and William Parker to Governor Clark, 1 August 1816, ibid., 15:180–82; Strickland, "Miller County," 15–19.

53. Fowler to McKinney, 14 April 1817, Natchitoches Letter Book, frame 55; Jamison to Secretary of War, 31 March 1817, in Carter, ed., *Territorial Papers* 15:257; Jamison to Secretary of War, 10 May 1817, *Territorial Papers* 15:302; Jamison to Secretary of War, 16 June 1819, ibid., 19:77; McKinney to Secretary of War, 16 July 1819, ibid., 19:86; Delegate J. W. Bates to Secretary of War, 27 November 1820, ibid., 19:237–39; Miller to Secretary of War, 11 December 1820, ibid., 19:244–46; "Account of United States Marshall," ibid., 19:458.

54. J. Villasana Haggard, "The Neutral Ground Between Louisiana and Texas," *Louisiana Historical Quarterly* 28 (1945): 1043ff; Odie B. Faulk,

"The Penetration of Foreigners and Foreign Ideas into Spanish East Texas," *East Texas Historical Journal* 2 (1964): 91–92.

55. Adams-Onís Treaty, in William M. Malloy, comp., *Treaties, Conventions, International Acts, Protocols, and Agreements between the United States and other Powers, 1776–1937,* 2:345. The boundaries were assigned as follows: from the mouth of the Sabine River (at present-day Sabine, Texas), up the west bank of the Sabine to its intersection with the 32d parallel; thence due north to the Red River and along its south bank to the 100th meridian; up that line to the Arkansas River; up the south bank of the Arkansas to its headwaters; thence due north to the 42d parallel, and along that line to the Pacific Ocean.

56. Fowler to McKinney, 4 July 1818, Natchitoches Letter Book, frame 73.

57. Ibid.

58. Ibid., 14 June 1819, frame 83.

59. Ibid., Fowler to Captain Robert S. Coomby, 29 December 1819, frame 87.

60. Ibid., Fowler to McKinney, 2 July 1819, frame 85.

61. Grand Jury Presentation in Hempstead County, April, 1920, LROSW, Roll 3, frame 958ff.

62. "Extract of a Letter to Governor Miller, 18 June 1820," in *Arkansas Gazette,* 15 July 1820.

63. Ibid., "Cherokee Chiefs to Governor Miller, 18 June 1820."

64. Ibid.

65. Swanton, *Indians,* 9; Dee Ann Suhm, Alex D. Krieger, and Edward B. Jelks, *An Introductory Handbook of Texas Archeology, Bulletin* 25, *Texas Archeological Society,* 144.

66. Suhm, Krieger, and Jelks, *Handbook,* 144, 152–62; John E. Swanton, *Source Material on the History and Ethnology of the Caddo Indians,* BAE Bulletin No. 132, 99ff. See also Herbert E. Bolton, *Texas in the Middle Eighteenth Century* (Berkeley: University of California Press, 1915), which delineates Spain's unsuccessful attempts to fortify east Texas as a barrier to French expansion.

67. Sibley, *Report from Natchitoches,* 95–96; Padilla, "Report," 47–49; Morse, *Report,* 373–74; Swanton, *Source Material on the Caddo,* 99ff.

68. Padilla, "Report," 47–49; Morse, *Report,* 373; Antonio Martínez to José Navarro, 4 April 1821, BA; Newcomb, *Indians of Texas,* 280.

69. Morse, *Report,* 374; Padilla, "Report," 49, 58; Newcomb, *Indians of Texas,* 274ff; Elizabeth Ann Harper, "The Taovayas Indians in Frontier Trade and Diplomacy, 1779–1835," *Panhandle-Plains Historical Review* 26 (1953): 58–61. See also Elizabeth A. H. John, *Storms Brewed in Other Men's Worlds: The Confrontation of Indians, Spanish, and French in the Southwest, 1540–1795,* for a discussion of the Wichitan peoples and their relationship with the French, the Spanish, and with other Texas tribes of the eighteenth century.

70. Antonio Martínez to Joaquín de Arredondo, Commandant-General of the Eastern Internal Provinces, 26 January 1819, in Virginia H. Taylor, ed.,

The Letters of Antonio Martínez, Last Spanish Governor of Texas, 1817–1822, 204; Martínez to Arredondo, 2 October 1819, ibid.; Martínez to José Antonio Navarro, 4 April 1821, BA. For the history and ethnography of the Comanches, see Ernest Wallace and E. Adamson Hoebel, *The Comanches: Lords of the South Plains.*

71. Sibley, *Report from Nachitoches,* 95–96.

72. Swanton, *Indians,* 145.

73. Morse, *Report,* 377; Padilla, "Report," 50; John Sibley to General Armstrong, 20 July 1814, in Julia K. Garrett, ed., "Doctor John Sibley and the Louisiana-Texas Frontier, 1804–1814," *Southwestern Historical Quarterly* 49 (1946): 605; Sibley to General Armstrong, 10 August 1814, in Garrett, ed., "Doctor John Sibley," 606–7.

74. Harry M. Henderson, "The Magee-Gutiérrez Expedition," *Southwestern Historical Quarterly* 55 (1951): 43–61.

75. Faulk, "Penetration of Foreigners," 92; Mattie Austin Hatcher, *The Opening of Texas to Foreign Settlement, 1801–1821,* University of Texas Bulletin No. 2714, 103; W. B. Bates, "A Sketch History of Nacogdoches," *Southwestern Historical Quarterly* 54 (1955): 491–97.

76. Reagan, *Memoirs,* 30–31.

2. *"What Is to Be Done with Us Poor Indians?"*

1. Governor José Felix Trespalacios to Gaspar López, 8 November 1822, BA.

2. Governor Antonio Martínez to José Navarro, 4 April 1821, BA.

3. Gaspar López to Antonio Martínez, 5 November 1821, BA.

4. Fields to Meigs, 25 September 1801, RCAT, Roll 1, #568; *Niles Weekly Register,* 19 September 1812; Starr, *History of the Cherokee Indians,* 467. Fields was a great-grandson of Ludovic Grant, a Scottish trader who had married a Cherokee woman in the early eighteenth century. In the early years of the nineteenth century Fields and his family had taken up land west of the Mississippi River. In 1804 he had filed claim on 640 acres southwest of the lower St. Francis River, somewhere near present-day Helena, Arkansas. At the same time his brother John filed on a 640-acre tract near New Madrid, Missouri, and his father-in-law, Francois Grappe, a trader at Nachitoches, filed on a similar parcel along the Black River in Louisiana (Starr, *History of the Cherokee Indians,* 305–6; *American State Papers, Claims* 36:360, 366; *Arkansas Gazette,* 2 September 1820). While Fields owned land west of the Mississippi as early as 1804, he may not have lived on it until later. The exact year of Fields's westward migration is unknown; his name does not appear in documents relating to the Arkansas Cherokees. The records indicate that he was still serving as a diplomat and warrior east of the Mississippi as late as 1814. He may have come directly to Texas, perhaps as early as 1819 or 1820.

5. *Niles Weekly Register,* 19 September 1812; Starr, *Cherokee Indians,* 467.

6. White, in Cherokee color symbolism, signified peace; red signified success (James Mooney, *Sacred Formulas of the Cherokees, Seventh Annual Report of the Bureau of American Ethnology, 1885–1886,* 342–43.

In peacetime Cherokees met frequently in the village council house to discuss business and take part in ceremonies. Seating was arranged according to clan affiliation. Assisting the peace chief, or "uku," were seven councillors, including a "right-hand man" and seven of the oldest and wisest of the tribe, one elder from each of the seven clans. The remaining body of men were an advisory body. In peacetime the white council worked as a task group in controlling local affairs. Their various functions included organizing repair of public buildings, clearing of new fields, and relocating the village. They also exercised social control by serving as a court. In addition, the council determined the proper time for holding ceremonies. And, as several ceremonies related directly to planting and harvesting, the council appointed the times for these endeavors. The peace organization also functioned in the debate over diplomatic matters. Any man or woman might speak in the debate. Although the "uku" might hold definite opinions favoring or opposing the issue, he had no control or coercive power and could only attempt to persuade. After the debate, the chief and the councillors would reconcile all of the opinions and indicate that a consensus had been reached. The decision would be announced, and thereafter no minority opinion would be expressed, although a faction in disagreement could elect nonparticipation in any action. Should the consensus be for diplomatic negotiation or war, the "red" organization, consisting of a war chief, his right-hand man, seven war councillors, a war speaker, and a surgeon, assumed the management of affairs (Gearing, "The Structural Poses of Eighteenth Century Cherokee Villages," 1152–53; Gilbert, *The Eastern Cherokees,* 321–23, 325–27, 348–49; Strickland, *Fire and the Spirits,* 24–26, 36–37; Gearing, *Priests and Warriors,* 23, 42, 47). The principle of moiety, or division, continued to function well into the nineteenth century, although its practical aspects were more obviously in evidence among the Arkansas and Texas Cherokees than among their kinsmen in the east.

7. Fields to Martínez, 1 February 1822, BA.

8. Trespalacios to Gaspar López, 8 November 1822, BA; Trespalacios to Kunetand, 9 November 1822, BA. In 1776 Spain's northern provinces, consisting of the present Mexican states of Sonora, Sinaloa, Chihuahua, Coahuila, Nuevo León, and Tamaulipas, and the portion of the present United States between California and Texas, were organized into a military district called the *Provincias Internas,* or Interior Provinces. The Interior Provinces were divided several times into separate administrative regions, but from 1813 onward Coahuila and Texas were part of a district known as the Eastern Interior Provinces. In 1820 Texas, Coahuila, Nuevo León, and Tamaulipas were the Eastern Interior Provinces. The administrator of this region was customarily a military commander based at Monterrey. In 1822 Colonel Mariano de Urrea and Colonel Antonio Cordéro functioned as commanders. Cordéro was followed in March 1823 by Colonel Gaspar de

Ochoa, who functioned in this capacity until mid-1824. After the adoption of the constitution of the Republic of Mexico in 1824, the northeastern region remained a military jurisdiction under the Mexican government. (Vigness, *The Revolutionary Decades,* 25–26; Thomas C. Barnes, et al., *Northern New Spain: A Research Guide,* 61–65, 114–15.)

9. Trespalacios to Gaspar López, 8 November 1822, BA. From the tone of this document, it appears that Fields had not represented himself as the Cherokees' headman. It would have been typical for the Mexican officials to demand the name of someone who was "in charge" of the Texas Cherokees, and Fields and the other members of his delegation may have supplied the name of another member of the council of elders. The delegation would not have been so bold as to name a new peace chief; that could only be done by the council, with a consensus of all the people. Or, from another viewpoint, these circumstances may indicate that Duwali was not in accord with the movement to negotiate, and that he may have been temporarily supplanted by "Kunetand," or more properly, Kanati. Kanati was originally from a town called Tellico; he had emigrated to Arkansas around 1797. It is possible that he may have been one of the Arkansas chiefs who moved his people to the Red River valley in 1820 (Treat to Dearborn, 2 April 1807, Letter Book of the Arkansas Trading House, 171; Kanati to Meigs, 17 June 1811, RCAT, Roll 5, #2667; Kanati to Meigs, 23 June 1811, RCAT, Roll 5, #2521).

Ernest Winkler, in his article on "The Cherokees in Texas," alleges that Duwali (Bowl) went to Mexico City with Fields. Winkler's source is a proclamation made by Governor Veramendi for Duwali and other Cherokees who were in Saltillo in August 1833. Read out of context, the wording of this document in Spanish would seem to imply that "Boles" and Richard Fields were in Mexico City together in 1822 (Veramendi Proclamation, 21 August 1833, General Land Office, Records and Archives Division, Spanish Archives, Appendix to Translations of Empresario Contracts, 3:300 [hereafter cited as ATEC]). The sentence reads, "those they represent have lived many years in that part of the state without being bothered, with permission of the Supreme Government generally conceded in the City of Mexico to the aforementioned Boles and Richard Fields." It is highly unlikely that Duwali actually went to Mexico City, given his advanced age and his civil, rather than diplomatic, status as primary chief. In 1833, however, Duwali may well have told Veramendi that the concession was made to him personally, given the death of Fields.

10. Trespalacios to Gaspar López, 8 November 1822, BA.

11. López to Trespalacios, 14 December 1822, BA.

12. H. P. N. Gammel, *The Laws of Texas, 1822–1897,* 1:27–30.

13. Henry Bamford Parkes, *History of Mexico,* 182–87.

14. Guzman to de la Garza, 27 April 1823, General Land Office of Texas, Records and Archives Division, Spanish Archives, Record of Translations of Empresario Contracts (hereafter referred to as RTEC), 86; Alamán to Saucedo, 18 September 1824, RTEC, 86–87.

15. Luciano García to Felix de la Garza, 22 July 1823, BA.
16. Bustamante to Trespalacios, 23 August 1822, BA; Santiago Dil (James Dill) to Trespalacios, 27 August 1822, BA.
17. Lester G. Bugbee, "The Texas Frontier, 1820–1825," *Proceedings of the Southern Historical Association* 4 (1929): 102–21.
18. Torres to Saucedo, 11 September 1824, BA.
19. Antonio Martínez to Joaquín de Arredondo, Commandant General of the Eastern Interior Provinces, 26 January 1819, in Taylor, ed., *Letters of Martínez,* 204; Martínez to Arredondo, 2 October 1819, ibid., Martínez to José Antonio Navarro, 4 April 1821, BA; Wallace and Hoebel, *The Comanches* 14, 287; Newcomb, *The Indians of Texas,* 157–58.
20. Fields to Saucedo, 6 March 1824, BA.
21. Ibid.
22. Gammel, *Laws of Texas* 1:97–98; Mary Virginia Henderson, "Minor Empresario Contracts for the Colonization of Texas, 1825–1834," *Southwestern Historical Quarterly* 31 (1928): 296.
23. Gammel, *Laws of Texas* 1:97–102; Mary Virginia Henderson, "Minor Empresario Contracts," 31 (1928): 296–300.
24. Contract for Colonization, RTEC, 23, 40, 158; Mary Virginia Henderson, "Minor Empresario Contracts for the Colonization of Texas," *Southwestern Historical Quarterly* 32 (1928): 16.
25. Fields to Commandant Juan Seguin, 12 August 1824, Nacogdoches Archives (hereafter cited as NA).
26. Fields to Saucedo, 1 September 1824, ATEC, 3:256–66. At the close of this letter Fields styled himself "Capt Gen Indian Tribes."
27. Gray to Secretary of War, April 1824, in Carter, ed., *Territorial Papers* 19:664.
28. Matthew Lyon to Secretary of War, 20 October 1821, in Carter, ed., *Territorial Papers* 19:330–40; Bradford to Secretary of War, 20 November 1821, ibid., 19:356; Miller to Secretary of War, May 1822, ibid., 19:437; Arbuckle to Adjutant General, 30 September 1822, ibid., 19:462; Secretary of War to Miller, 9 December 1822, ibid., 19:472; Acting Governor Crittendon to Secretary of War, 28 September 1823, ibid., 19:546–48.
29. Arbuckle to Morse, Acting Adjutant General, 3 September 1823, in Carter, ed., *Territorial Papers* 19:545.
30. Ibid., Crittenden to Secretary of War, 28 September 1823, 19:546–48.
31. Ibid.; Secretary of War to John Cocke, 12 January 1824, in Carter, ed., *Territorial Papers* 19:591.
32. Washburn, *Reminiscences,* 165; John Jolly to Edward Duval, 4 December 1825, in Carter, ed., *Territorial Papers* 20:319; Markman, "The Arkansas Cherokees," 110.
33. John Jolly to Edward Duval, 4 December 1826, in Carter, ed., *Territorial Papers* 20:319.
34. Major Alexander Cummings to Adjutant General, 18 January 1826, in Carter, ed., *Territorial Papers* 20:184–85; Col. Matthew Arbuckle to E. G. W. Butler, Adjutant General, 4 November 1826, Carter, ed., *Territorial Papers*

20:301–2; Duval to William Clark, 6 December 1826, LROSW, Roll 77, #0248.

35. Edmund C. Shoemaker, "Fort Towson: An Early Communications Route to Oklahoma," *Red River Valley Historical Review* 7 (1982): 18–24; John Ridge, "The Cherokee War Path," ed. Carolyn Foreman, *Chronicles of Oklahoma* 9 (1931): 238–39 (narrative of John Smith as told to John Ridge in 1836).

36. Saucedo to Alamán, 20 August 1824, BA.

37. Alamán to Saucedo, 18 September 1824, ATEC, 3:137.

38. Fields to Saucedo, 22 April 1825, NA.

39. Austin to Saucedo, 8 September 1825, BA; Austin to Ahumada, 10 September 1825, in Eugene C. Barker, ed., *The Austin Papers* 1:1197; Austin's Address, "Referendum on Indian Relations, 28 September 1825, in Barker, ed., *Austin Papers* 1:1208–11.

40. Austin to Ahumada, 10 September 1825, in Barker, ed., *Austin Papers* 1:1197; Ahumada to Elosua, 30 October 1825, BA; Ahumada to Saucedo, 10 November 1825, BA.

41. Purnell to Fields, 4 October 1825, in Barker, ed., *Austin Papers* 1:1220.

42. Durcy to Grappe, 10 November 1825, in Barker, ed., *Austin Papers* 1:1231–32.

43. Richard Drinnon, *White Savage: The Case of John Dunn Hunter,* 174; Ernest W. Winkler, "The Cherokee Indians in Texas," *Quarterly of the Texas State Historical Association* 7 (1903): 121–22.

44. Drinnon, *White Savage,* 182; Winkler, "The Cherokee Indians," 122.

45. Drinnon, *White Savage,* 182–83.

46. Peter Ellis Bean to Austin, 31 December 1826, in Barker, ed., *Austin Papers* 1:1554.

47. Saucedo to Alcalde, 2 February 1826, NA; Arciniega Diary, Appendix to Empresario Contracts, 55:272.

48. Norris to Ahumada, 8 July 1826, BA.

49. Cummings to Jones, January 18, 1826, in Carter, ed., *Territorial Papers* 20:195; Kappler, comp., *Indian Affairs: Laws* 2:211–14 (Choctaw), 217–21 (Osage), 222–24 (Kansa), 248–50 (Kansa), 262–64 (Shawnee), 273–76 (Potawatamie), 276–80 (Miami), 303–5 (Delaware, 1829).

50. Archivo General de México, Colonización (Transcripts in Texas State Library, Archives Division), Legajo 4, Expediente 21; the RTEC also contain extensive documentation concerning the Shawnees' settlement.

51. Saucedo to Alcalde of Nacogdoches, 12 February 1826, NA.

52. Gonzales to Secretary of War, 14 November 1825, RTEC, 87–88; Gonzales to Saucedo, 27 December 1825, RTEC, 88.

53. Arciniega Diary, ATEC, 55:272.

54. Fields to Saucedo, 20 March 1826, NA.

55. Saucedo to Fields, 3 May 1826, BA.

56. Ahumada to Austin, 10 April 1826, BA.

57. Austin to Richard Fields, 26 April 1826, in Barker, ed., *Austin Papers* 1:1307–9.

58. Ibid., Austin to Ahumada, 30 April 1826, 1:1315–17.
59. Ibid., Austin to Ross, 13 May 1826, 1:1338.
60. Ibid., Austin to Ahumada, 8 May 1826, 1:1323.
61. Norris to Saucedo, 22 March 1826, NA; Sepulveda to Saucedo, 23 March 1826, NA; Saucedo to Norris, 28 March 1826, NA; Ahumada to Saucedo, 2 April 1826, NA; Norris to Saucedo, 4 April 1826, NA; List of Ranchos not to be Interfered with by Haden Edwards, 20 April 1826, NA; Norris to Saucedo, NA; Saucedo's Proclamation, 17 May 1826, NA; Edmund Morris Parsons, "The Fredonian Rebellion," *Texana* 5 (1967): 13–15.
62. Order to Arrest Haden Edwards, 18 May 1826, NA; Vigness, *Revolutionary Decades* 79; Parsons, "Fredonian Rebellion," 14.
63. Edwards to Austin, 21 July 1826, in Barker, ed., *Austin Papers* 1:1384–85; Drinnon, *White Savage,* 194–96; Winkler, "Cherokee Indians," 130–33.
64. Norris to Saucedo, 22 August 1826, NA; Norris to Saucedo, 5 September 1826, NA; Norris to Saucedo, 17 October 1826; NA. Edwards's contract originally called for the introduction of eight hundred families.
65. Fields to Austin, ca. 5 September 1826, NA.
66. Fields to Norris, ca. 5 September 1826, NA.
67. Austin to Saucedo, 11 September 1826, NA.
68. Notice by Saucedo, 20 September 1826, NA.
69. Sepulveda to Saucedo, 13 November 1826, NA; Sepulveda to Saucedo, 28 November 1826, NA; Alcalde Norris to Saucedo, 28 November 1826, NA; Sepulveda to Saucedo, 3 December 1826; NA; Austin to Saucedo, 4 December 1826, NA; Parsons, "Fredonian Rebellion," 15–21, 23–24.
70. Sepulveda to Saucedo, 13 November 1826, NA; Bean to Austin, 23 December 1826, Saltillo Archives (Transcripts, Barker Texas History Collection, University of Texas, Austin); Drinnon, *White Savage,* 204–6.
71. Bean to Austin, 31 December 1826, in Barker, ed., *Austin Papers* 1:1553.
72. Fredonian Declaration, 21 December 1826, NA; B. W. Edwards and H. B. May to the Inhabitants of Pecan Point, 25 December 1826, in Barker, ed., *Austin Papers* 1:1542–44; Austin to Saucedo, 4 January 1827, Saltillo Archives, Legajo 19, Expediente 190.
73. Bean to Austin, 23 December 1826, Saltillo Archives, Legajo 19, Expediente 190; Bean to Austin, 31 December 1826, in Barker, *Austin Papers* 1:1553.
74. Saucedo to Fields, 4 January 1827, in Barker, ed., *Austin Papers* 1:1563–1564.
75. Austin to Cherokee Chiefs, 24 January 1827, in ibid., 1:1592–94.
76. Amnesty Proclamation, 6 January 1827, NA; Ellis, Cummins, and Kerr to Austin, 22 January 1827, in Barker, ed., *Austin Papers* 1:1586–87.
77. Bean to Fields, 4 January 1827, NA; Bean to Austin, 4 January 1827, in Barker, ed., *Austin Papers* 1:1561; Bean to Ahumada, 7 February 1827, NA.
78. Parsons, "Fredonian Rebellion," 46.
79. Strickland, *Fire and the Spirits,* 37.
80. "Information Derived from Col. Hayden Edwards," in Charles A.

Gulick et al., eds., *The Papers of Mirabeau Buonaparte Lamar* 3:263.

81. Bean to Ahumada, 7 February 1827, NA; Francisco Ruíz to Ahumada, 14 May 1827, NA.

82. Saucedo to Arispe, 15 March 1827, BA; Ahumada to Bustamante, 1 March 1827, BA.

83. Bustamante to Ahumada, 20 March 1827, NA.

84. Bustamante to Ahumada, 7 April 1827, NA.

3. The Calm: Hopeful Accommodation, 1828–1835

1. Ohland Morton, "Life of General Don Manuel Mier y Terán, as It Affected Texas-Mexican Relations," *Southwestern Historical Quarterly* 47 (1943): 122–28; Alleine Houren, "The Causes and Origin of the Decree of April 6, 1830," *Southwestern Historical Quarterly* 16 (1913): 395–98.

2. José María Sánchez, "A Trip to Texas in 1828," trans. Carlos Castañeda, *Southwestern Historical Quarterly* 29 (1926): 286.

3. Douglas C. Wilms, "Cherokee Acculturation and Changing Land Use Practices," *Chronicles of Oklahoma* 61 (1978): 335.

4. Kiamee's Statement, Meigs to Secretary of War, 6 April 1811, RCAT, Roll 5, #2627.

5. Petition of Cherokee Chiefs, 18 July 1833, RTEC, 283.

6. Austin to Madero, 11 November 1827, in Barker, ed., *Austin Papers* 2:1721; Sánchez, "Trip," 283; Thorn to Austin, 22 July 1828, in Barker, ed., *Austin Papers* 2:74; Jean Louis Berlandier, *The Indians of Texas in 1830*, ed. John C. Ewers, trans. Patricia R. Leclercq, 113.

7. Albert Woldert, "The Last of the Cherokees in Texas and the Life and Death of Chief Bowles, *Chronicles of Oklahoma* 1 (June 1923): 193ff.

8. Ibid., 101.

9. Fields to Saucedo, 6 March 1823, BA; Fields to Procela, 27 April 1825, NA. For the cultural configurations of east Texas as determined by archeological investigations, see Suhm, Krieger, and Jelks, *The Handbook of Texas Archeology;* E. M. Davis, "The Caddoan Area," *Bulletin of the Texas Archeological Society* 31 (1960); A. D. Kreiger, *Culture Complexes and Chronology in Northern Texas,* University of Texas Publication 4640; S. A. Skinner, *Historical Archeology of the Neches Saline in Smith County, Texas,* THSC Archeological Report No. 21; and Clarence Webb, "A Review of Northeast Texas Archeology," *Bulletin of the Texas Archeological Society* 29 (1960). Despite numerous excavations in the region of east Texas, little has been revealed concerning the Cherokees' occupation. It may well be that in the historic period (including the early nineteenth century) the durable aspects of the Cherokees' material culture (metal, ceramics, and house sites) were so similar to those of contemporary and later Hispanic and American occupants that no real differences can be distinguished.

10. Ben Milam, Agent of General Wavell, to Commandant of Texas, 1 May 1827, ATEC, 55:16–17; Sánchez, "Trip," 286; Burnet to Bustamente, July 2, 1827, in Barker, ed., *Austin Papers* 1:1667.

11. Sánchez, "Trip," 288; Woldert, "Last of the Cherokees in Texas," 194.
12. Sánchez, "Trip," 286; Berlandier, *Indians,* 113; Mary Virginia Henderson, "Minor Empresario Contracts," 31 (1928): 295.
13. John Jolly to Edward Duval, 4 December 1826, in Carter, ed., *Territorial Papers* 20:319; Carolyn Foreman, "Dutch," *Chronicles of Oklahoma* 28 (1949): 255.
14. Washburn, *Reminiscences,* 175; Mooney, *Myths,* 141.
15. Petition of Cherokees, 18 July 1833, ATEC, 55:283; Juan N. Almonte, *Noticia Estadística Sobre Tejas,* 87; Almonte, *Noticia Estadística,* Chart 3.
16. Swanton, *Indians,* 244–49.
17. Nuttall, *Journal* 13:194; Washburn, *Reminiscences,* 17; George Vashon to John Eaton, 6 November 1830, Records of the Bureau of Indian Affairs, Correspondence of the Office of Indian Affairs, Letters Received, 1824–1881, Cherokee Agency West, Microfilm M234, Roll 77, frame 0635 (hereafter referred to as Cherokee Agency West, roll number, frame number).
18. Sánchez, "Trip," 283; Swanton, *Indians,* 244–49.
19. Meigs's Journal of Occurrences, 1801, RCAT, Roll 1, no #; Charles A. Amsden, *Navaho Weaving: Its Technic and Its History,* 21.
20. Antonio Bulfe (Wolfe?), in letter of Alcalde of Nacogdoches to Political Chief, 11 September 1824, BA.
21. Sánchez, "Trip," 283; Swanton, *Indians,* 244–49.
22. Thorn to Austin, 22 July 1828, in Barker, ed., *Austin Papers* 2:74.
23. Albert Woldert, *A History of Tyler and Smith County, Texas,* 10; Houston to Martin Lacy, 17 September 1836, in Amelia W. Williams and Eugene C. Barker, eds., *The Writings of Sam Houston, 1813–1863,* 1:446.
24. Berlandier, *Indians,* 49, 94; Jim Bowie to Henry Rueg, 3 August 1835, in John H. Jenkins, ed., *Papers of the Texas Revolution* 1:301–2.
25. Swanton, *Indians,* 386, 403, 806; Hudson, *Southeastern Indians,* 213–16.
26. Nuttall, *Journal* 13:172–73, 192ff.; Swanton, *Indians,* 386, 403, 806; Hudson, *Southeastern Indians,* 213–16.
27. Berlandier, *Indians,* 44.
28. Thorn to Austin, 22 July 1828, in Barker, ed., *Austin Papers* 2:72.
29. Gearing, "Structural Poses, 1149.
30. Thorn to Austin, 22 July 1828, in Barker, ed., *Austin Papers* 2:72.
31. Sánchez, "Trip," 286–87.
32. Gilbert, *Eastern Cherokees,* 336; Hudson, *Southeastern Indians,* 240–70.
33. Gilbert, *Eastern Cherokees,* 330; Bloom, "Acculturation," 331.
34. Gilbert, *Eastern Cherokees,* 334.
35. Ibid., 326–27, 334.
36. Gearing, *Priests and Warriors,* 103–4; Gilbert, *Eastern Cherokees,* 367–68; Swanton, *Indians,* 771–72.
37. Berlandier, *Indians,* 94; Jim Bowie to Henry Rueg, 3 August 1835, in Jenkins, ed., *Papers of the Texas Revolution* 1:301–2.
38. McLoughlin, *Cherokees and Missionaries,* 341–42.

39. Sánchez, "Trip," 288.
40. Berlandier, *Indians,* 52.
41. Ibid., 49
42. Ibid., plate 9; Ridge, "Cherokee War Path," 240.
43. Hudson, *Southeastern Indians,* 264; Mooney, *Myths,* plates 4 and 6.
44. Sánchez, "Trip," 286; Almonte to Governor of Coahuila and Texas, 16 June 1834, Spanish Archives, Transcripts, Eugene C. Barker Texas History Collection, Legajo 29, Expediente 1302.
45. Berlandier, *Indians,* 112.
46. Ibid., 39.
47. Colonel Boles, John Boles, Richard Jestice, Piggion, Andrew M. Vann, and Eli Harlin to Miguel Arciniega, 16 July 1833, RTEC, 55:286 (this document is written in Spanish, but appended to it is one page which appears to be written phonetically, in Cherokee); Mush to Nacogdoches Committee of Safety, 13 April 1836, Andrew Jackson Houston Papers, (hereafter cited as AJHP), No. 368 (this document is in English, but sixteen lines of Cherokee syllabary script are written on the reverse; see illustration in text above.
48. Berlandier, *Indians,* 39.
49. Juan Almonte to Governor of Texas, 16 June 1834, Spanish Archives, Legajo 29, Expediente 1302, 8–13; Foreman, "Cherokee War Path," 240–41.
50. Sánchez, "Trip," 286–88; Mooney, *Sacred Formulas of the Cherokees,* 468.
51. Sánchez, "Trip," 288.
52. Edward Duval to William Clark, 6 December 1826, in Carter, ed., *Territorial Papers,* 20:310–20; William Clark to Secretary of War, 6 January 1827, ibid., 20:357–58; William Clark to Secretary of War, 2 March 1827, ibid., 20:410.
53. Colonel Matthew Arbuckle to Bates, 26 March 1827, Cherokee Agency, West, Roll 77, frame 0291; Foreman, *Indians and Pioneers,* 249.
54. Rabb to Austin, 24 November 1828, in Barker, ed., *Austin Papers* 2:1445; Austin to José Antonio Navarro, 23 July 1829, in Barker, ed., *Austin Papers* 2:233–35; Sánchez, "Trip," 279; Foreman, "Cherokee War Path," 253–60.
55. Morton, "Life of General Don Manuel Mier y Terán," 122–40.
56. Terán to Victoria, 30 June 1828, in Houren, "The Causes and Origin of the Decree of April 6, 1830," 406–13; *Texas Gazette,* July 3, 1830.
57. Henderson, "Minor Empresario Contracts," 32(1928):16.
58. Thorn to Austin, 22 July 1828, in Barker, ed., *Austin Papers* 2:74–75.
59. Contract, 23 December 1826, RTEC, 121–23; Contract, October, 1831, RTEC, 192–93.
60. Letona to Commandant General, 1 September 1831, in Dorman H. Winfrey and James M. Day, eds., *The Texas Indian Papers, 1825–1916* 1:2.
61. Ibid.
62. Ibid., Musquiz to Letona, 25 September 1831, 1:2–3.
63. Ibid., Letona to Musquiz, 22 March 1832, 1:4, Musquiz to Letona, 22 April 1832, ibid., 1:4.

64. Fogelson and Kutsche, "Cherokee Economic Cooperatives," 87; Bloom, "Acculturation," 326; Perdue, *Slavery and the Evolution of Cherokee Society,* 14, 33, 55; Reid, *Law of Blood,* 191–94; Strickland, *Fire and the Spirits,* 95–97.

65. Edna Rowe, "The Disturbance at Anahuac in 1832," *Southwestern Historical Quarterly* 6 (1903):265–99; Eugene C. Barker, "The Battle of Velasco," *Southwestern Historical Quarterly* 7 (1903):326–28.

66. Bullock to Alcalde of San Felipe, 9 August 1832, quoted in John Henry Brown, *History of Texas* (St. Louis, Mo.: 1892–1893), 192 n.

67. Frost Thorn to Austin, 28 August 1832, in Barker, ed., *Austin Papers* 2:851.

68. Parkes, *A History of Mexico,* 201–2.

69. Ibid., 202; William C. Binckley, *The Texas Revolution,* 8–9.

70. Political Chief to Governor, 20 July 1833, RTEC, 278–81.

71. Petition of Cherokees, 18 July 1833, RTEC, 283.

72. Ibid.

73. Ibid., 284.

74. Bean to Elosua, 7 October 1833, ATEC, 55:287; Elosua to Arciniega, 23 October 1833, ATEC, 55:291–93.

75. Arciniega to Elosua, 23 October 1833, ATEC, 55:295; Arciniega to Alcalde of Nacogdoches, 24 October 1833, ATEC, 55:297; Jose Ybarbo, Alcalde of Nacogdoches, to Arciniega, 19 November 1833, ATEC, 55:298.

76. Copy of Beramendi's Decree, 21 August 1833, ATEC, 55:300–301.

77. Censuses of the Nacogdoches Area, Records of the States of the United States of America, Nacogdoches Archives, 1828–1836, Microfilm, Roll 16, no document number.

78. Henderson, "Empresario Grants," 313; *Abstract of All Original Texas Land Titles Comprising Grants and Locations to August 31, 1941,* 1:1–396. Burnet had sold his rights to the Galveston Bay and Texas Land Company.

79. Juan N. Almonte, "Statistical Report on Texas," ed. Carlos Castañeda, *Southwestern Historical Quarterly* 28 (1924):222; Helen Willits Harris, "Almonte's Inspection of Texas in 1834," *Southwestern Historical Quarterly* 41 (1938):205.

80. Binckley, *Texas Revolution,* 68–91; Eugene C. Barker, ed., "Journal of the Permanent Council, October 11 to 27, 1835," *Southwestern Historical Quarterly* 7 (1903):249–51.

81. Decree 192, ATEC, 55:60.

82. Deposition of A. Manchaca, 11 February 1835, NA; Ruiz to Alcalde of Nacogdoches, 16 February 1835, in Jenkins, ed., *Papers of the Texas Revolution* 1:46.

83. Ugartechea to Bean, 26 March 1835, in Jenkins, ed., *Papers of the Texas Revolution* 1:44; Bean to Ugartechea, 15 June 1835, ibid., 1:152.

84. Bowie to Rueg, 3 August 1835, in Jenkins, ed., *Papers of the Texas Revolution* 1:301–2.

85. Decree 313, 12 May 1835, Gammel, *Laws of Texas* 1:410.

86. Big Mush and Bowles's speech to the Cherokees, 19 September 1835,

in Gulick et al., eds., *Lamar Papers* 1:239; Houston and Rusk to Bowl and Big Mush, 24 September 1835, in Jenkins, ed., *Papers of the Texas Revolution* 1:486–87.

87. Llerena Friend, *Sam Houston, the Great Designer,* 5–9.

88. Jack Kilpatrick and Rennard Strickland, *Sam Houston with the Cherokees, 1829–1833* 17, 36, 104, 132–33, 144–48, 164.

89. Friend, *Sam Houston,* 35–36, 38.

90. Royall to Austin, 18 October 1835, in Jenkins, ed., *Papers of the Texas Revolution* 2:155–56; Royall to Austin, 19 October 1835, in Barker, ed., *Austin Papers* 3:192; Mosely Baker and Francis W. Johnson to Chairman of Council, 23 October 1835, in Jenkins, ed., *Papers of the Texas Revolution* 1:200–201.

91. Gammel, *Laws of Texas* 1:546–47.

92. Houston to Colonel Bowl, 22 November 1835, in Williams and Barker, eds., *Writings of Sam Houston* 3:7.

93. Menard to Council, 26 November 1835, in Jenkins, ed., *Papers of the Texas Revolution* 2:513.

94. Gammel, *Laws of Texas* 1:688.

95. Sam Houston to Henry Smith, 29 February 1836, in Williams and Barker, eds., *Writings of Sam Houston* 1:357.

96. Treaty of 1836, Records Relating to Indian Affairs (Texas State Library, Austin). "Unataqua" seems to be phonetically similar to Anadarko and presumably refers to that Caddoan tribe. "Tahocuttake" could be a corruption of Kadohadacho, which means "real Caddoes"; there had been an influx of Caddoes into Texas from Louisiana after 1835, when the Caddoes ceded their lands to the United States. They settled in the Great Bend of the Red River, in U.S. territory, and southwestward from there all the way to Nacogdoches. They would have been distinct from the Anadarkos, of the old Hasinai confederacy in Texas, and also from the "Caddo of the Neches." On the other hand, "Tahocuttake" could be a corruption of "Chikkihashachi," or Chickasaw. The Chickasaws had been drifting westward from Mississippi for decades, and in the 1830s they, too, had been making cession treaties. There was at least one village of Chickasaws in Texas in the late 1820s, and in the late 1830s there was a large one on Attoyac Bayou, outside the Cherokees' claim. In the Cherokee language, the closest word to "Tahocuttake" is Takatoka ("Standing Bear"); one historian has suggested that these may have been some of the Arkansas chief Takatoka's people residing in Texas, but surely these would not have been denoted as a separate group.

The names of Boles (Duwali), his son John Boles, Big Mush (Gatunwali), Benge, and Tunnetee (Kanati) appear regularly in records relating to the Cherokees in Texas. Oosoota (Utsidihi, or "Mankiller") and Corn Tassel (Utsitsata) are also common Cherokee names. Names of the chiefs of the other tribes were seldom noted in the records, but in the mid to late 1830s, the Shawnees were represented in conferences by, and addressed in correspondence to, "Linney" and "Spy Buck"; the Delawares by "Harris"; the Kickapoos by "Benido"; the Biloxis by "Antonio"; the Coushattas by "Benash"; and the Caddoes by "Coloxe."

97. Sam Houston to Henry Smith, 29 February 1836, in Williams and Barker, eds., *Writings of Sam Houston* 1:357.
98. Ibid.; Ernest W. Winkler, ed., *Secret Journals of the Senate of the Republic of Texas, 1836–1845,* 36–39.
99. R. Earl McClendon, "The First Treaty of the Republic of Texas," *Southwestern Historical Quarterly* 52 (1948):32–48.

4. The Storm: Revolution and Rebellion, 1836–1838

1. Henry Smith to Convention, March 1, 1836, in Jenkins, ed., *Papers of the Texas Revolution* 4:483; McClendon, "First Treaty of the Republic of Texas," 36.
2. Santa Ana to Tornel, 16 February 1836, in Jenkins, ed., *Papers of the Texas Revolution* 4:361.
3. General E. P. Gaines to Lewis Cass, 8 April 1836, reprinted in *Telegraph and Texas Register,* 6 September 1836; Deposition of Cortinez, 12 April 1836, in Jenkins, ed., *Papers of the Texas Revolution* 4:446.
4. Mexican Consulate in New Orleans to Manual Flores, "Commissionado por el Gran Jefe Caddo," 25 November 1835, Thomas Jefferson Rusk Papers, Folder 1; Report of Lt. Bonnell to General Gaines, 20 April 1836, H. Doc. 351, 25th Cong., 2d sess., 1838, 774–75.
5. M. B. Menard Deposition, 11 April 1836, AJHP, No. 0356; Anna Muckleroy, "The Indian Policy of the Republic of Texas," *Southwestern Historical Quarterly* 26 (1922):3–4, 6.
6. Vigness, *Revolutionary Decades,* 173–98; Binkley, *Texas Revolution,* 93–117.
7. John A. Quitman to Houston, 5 April 1836, in Jenkins, ed., *Papers of the Texas Revolution* 5:484.
8. Houston to Colonel Bowl, 13 April 1836, in Williams and Barker, eds., *The Writings of Sam Houston* 1:409.
9. William Parker to Editor of *Natchez Free Trader,* 29 April 1836, in Jenkins, ed., *Papers of the Texas Revolution* 6:119–20.
10. Big Mush to Committee of Safety, 13 April 1836, AJHP, No. 0368.
11. Robert L. Jones and Pauline Jones, "The Occupation of Nacogdoches," *East Texas Historical Journal* 2 (1964):24–27.
12. Deposition of Michael B. Menard, 11 April 1836, AJHP, No. 0356; Deposition of William Sims, 11 April 1836, H. Doc. 351, 776.
13. Sims Deposition, 11 April 1836, H. Doc. 351, 776; Henderson Yoakum, *History of Texas* 2:126; Carson to Burnet, 14 April 1836, in George P. Garrison, ed., *Diplomatic Correspondence of the Republic of Texas;* Parker to Editor, 29 April 1836, in Jenkins, ed., *Papers of the Texas Revolution* 6:119–20.
14. Captain J. Dean to Lt. Col. Vose, 10 May 1826, in Jenkins, ed., *Papers of the Texas Revolution* 6:203–4; James T. De Shields, *Cynthia Ann Parker: The Story of her Capture at the Massacre of the Inmates of Parker's Fort,* 12–16; Thomas M. Marshall, *History of the Western Boundary of the Louisiana Purchase, 1819–1841,* 174–75.
15. Edwards to Gaines, 13 May 1836, H. Doc. 351, 800–802; Felix Huston to

Secretary of War, 13 December 1836, S. Doc. 14, 32d Cong., 2d Sess. 1853, 37.

16. Secretary of Colonization to Secretary of War and Marine, 19 August 1836, Archivo General de Mexico (Transcripts, Texas State Library, Austin), Legajo 10, Expediente 86 (contains the text of Urrea's letter to the Secretary of War dated 19 July 1836).

17. Felix Huston to Secretary of War, 13 December 1836, S. Doc. 14, 37; James Douglas to Hon. William H. Wharton, 23 December 1838, S. Doc., 14, 40–41.

18. Jones, "Occupation," 28–29.

19. Menard to Houston, 9 August 1836, in Jenkins, ed., *Papers of the Texas Revolution* 8:177–79.

20. Pantallion's Report, 9 August 1836, H. Doc. 351, 802–3.

21. Pantallion's Report, 9 August 1836, H. Doc. 351, 802–3; later evidence suggests that there were Cherokees in Matamoros during the late autumn of 1836 and early winter of 1837 (Anthony Butler to Felix Huston, 21 December 1838, S. Doc. 14, 38–39).

22. Menard to Houston, 9 August 1836, in Jenkins, ed., *Papers of the Texas Revolution* 8:177–79.

23. Basques Deposition, 7 September 1836, H. Doc. 351, 819.

24. Houston to Gaines, 29 August 1836, AJHP, No. 0520; Friend, *Sam Houston,* 75.

25. "To the Citizens of Texas," 29 August 1836, in Williams and Barker, eds., *Writings of Sam Houston* 1:445–46.

26. Houston to Captain Michael Costley, 1 September 1836, in Williams and Barker, eds., *Writings of Sam Houston* 4:23.

27. Joseph Milton Nance, *After San Jacinto: The Texas-Mexican Frontier, 1836–1841,* 19–26.

28. Houston to Costley, 1 September 1836, in Williams and Barker, eds., *Writings of Sam Houston* 4:23; Friend, *Houston,* 76–77.

29. Houston to Costley, 17 September 1836, AJHP, No. 0547; Order to Captain of Cherokee Rangers, 23 September 1836, AJHP, No. 0548.

30. Houston to Martin Lacey, 17 September 1836, in Williams and Barker, eds., *Writings of Sam Houston* 1:446; Woldert, *History of Tyler and Smith County,* 10.

31. Anthony Butler to General Felix Huston, 21 December 1838, S. Doc. 14, 38–40.

32. Bowl to Houston, 14 January 1837, AJHP No. 0777 (this letter is signed "Teawully"); Houston to Bowl, 7 March 1838, AJHP, No. 0876; Rusk to Houston, 11 March 1837, AJHP, No. 0904.

33. Henry Millard to Houston, 23 March 1837, AJHP, No. 0939; Walker Reid to Houston, 29 March 1837, AJHP, No. 0959; Rusk to Houston, 8 May 1837, AJHP, No. 1050.

34. Lt. Bonnell to Authorities of Nacogdoches, 7 March 1837, AJHP, No. 0777.

35. Goyens to Houston, 22 March 1837, AJHP, No. 0933; Message of President Houston to the House and Senate, 5 May 1837, in *Telegraph and*

Texas Register, 9 May 1837; Irion to Hunt, 20 September 1837, in Garrison, ed., *Diplomatic Correspondence* 1:259–60.

36. D. W. Smith to John Forsyth, U.S. Department of State, Consular Despatches, Matamoros, Microfilm M281 (Washington, D.C.: 1954), Roll 2, no frame number; James Douglas to William H. Wharton, 23 December 1838, S. Doc. 14, 40–41.

37. William Goyens to Houston, 10 May 1837, reprinted in *Telegraph and Texas Register,* 12 January 1837.

38. Ibid.

39. Ibid.

40. Bowl to Rusk, 28 May 1837, Rusk Papers, Folder 1.

41. Houston to Rusk, 7 June 1837. Rusk Papers, Folder 1.

42. Houston to Rusk, 16 June 1837, Rusk Papers, Folder 1; Houston to Rusk, 27 June 1837, AJHP, No. 1214.

43. Houston to Bowl, 3 July 1837, in Gulick, ed., *Lamar Papers* 1:559; Houston to Goyens, 3 July 1837; in Gulick, ed., *Lamar Papers* 1:559.

44. Houston to Goyens, 23 July 1837, AJHP, No. 0800.

45. Muckleroy, "Indian Policy," 17–18.

46. Winkler, ed., *Secret Journals of the Senate,* 35–39; *Telegraph and Texas Register,* 9 May 1837.

47. Report of the Standing Committee on Indian Affairs, 12 October 1837, in Winfrey and Day, eds., *Texas Indian Papers* 4:22.

48. Ibid.

49. Ibid., 22–28; Winkler, ed., *Secret Journals of the Senate,* 101.

50. Thomas F. Miller, *The Public Lands of Texas, 1519–1970,* 9; *Abstracts of Original Titles in the General Land Office of Texas* 1:1–396; Houston to Texas Congress, 19 November 1838, in Williams and Barker, eds., *Writings of Sam Houston,* 2:299–300.

51. Houston to Texas Senate, 21 May 1838, in Williams and Barker, eds., *Writings of Sam Houston,* 4:60.

52. S. A. Maverick to Mary A. Maverick, April 28, 1838, in R. M. Green, ed., *Sam Maverick, Texan, 1803–1870: A Collection of Letters,* 68–70. Some examination is due Duwali's statement about having given a daughter to Houston for a wife. First, Houston's only documented Indian wife was Talihina (Diana) Rogers; however, various sources allege that Houston may have married a Cherokee girl during his 1809–1811 sojourn among the Cherokees of the Hiwassee River region in Tennessee (see Gregory and Strickland, *Sam Houston and the Cherokees*). Duwali was a chief in a Hiwassee village, and it could be that Houston married one of Duwali's daughters at this time.

Second, there is some question as to the exact meaning of the term "daughter" as used by the chief. In traditional Cherokee kinship terminology (assuming that this is the way he thought), several girls other than Duwali's biological female offspring would also have been called "daughter" by him, those persons being his brother's daughter, his father's brother's daughter, his mother's brother's daughter, and his mother's sister's daughter. Unfortunately, in Duwali's genealogy (contained in Emmet Starr's *History of the Cherokee Indians*) there is mention of neither his parentage nor his siblings; therefore, we do not know whether or how he might have been related to John Rogers, perhaps as a full or half brother (or even as an adoptive brother). It is interesting to note that in the genealogical tables of Starr, Talihina's mother (John Rogers's wife) was named Jennie Due; coincidentally, one of Duwali's three wives was named Jennie (the other two were Utsuta and Utiyu). It is possible (though perhaps barely probable) that Duwali married Jennie Due after the death of John Rogers, thereby becoming Talihina's "father." However, Starr does not mention any such connection. It should also be noted that among the Cherokees, marriages were easily dissolved and that serial and sororal polygyny were practiced (see Swanton, *Indians of the Southeastern United States,* for an explanation of kinship terminology and marriage customs among the various southeastern tribes). Gregory and Strickland also allege that Talihina was the niece of Talontuskee and John Jolly; perhaps there is a family connection among Duwali, Rogers, Talontuskee, and Jolly that could explain Duwali's application of the term "daughter" to Houston's wife.

The whole problem of Cherokee genealogy in the early nineteenth century is complicated by lack of documentary evidence and by the traditional matrilineal system of descent reckoning giving way to patrilineal (traditional European) reckoning because of an increasing number of marriages between Cherokees and outsiders of European ancestry (see Strickland, *Fire and the Spirits,* for a discussion of Cherokee marriage and inheritance law; see Robin Fox, *Kinship and Marriage: An Anthropological Perspective* [Middlesex, England: Penguin Books, 1967] for an examination of the complications of matrilineal and patrilineal kinship reckoning).

53. Jeff Wright (Cherokee Agent) to Houston, 17 June 1838, AJHP, No. 1683.

54. Foreman, "Dutch," 258.

55. Arbuckle to Jones, 30 May 1838; Records of the U.S. Army Continental Commands, Record Group 393. Fort Gibson Letterbooks, National Archives; Simmons to Vose, 30 May 1838, Fort Gibson Letterbooks.

56. Holland Coffee to General Felix Huston, 17 December 1838, S. Doc. 14, 38.

57. Woodward, *The Cherokees,* 204–18.

58. James Douglas to General Felix Huston, 23 December 1838, S. Doc. 14, 40–41.

59. "Private Instructions for the Captains of Friendly Indians of Texas, by His Excellency General-in-Chief Vicente Filisola" (1838?), S. Doc. 14, 13. General Vicente Filisola had been relieved of his command in June 1836 and had retired to Saltillo. His superiors were dissatisfied with his performance in Texas after the 21 April battle in San Jacinto. He was tried and imprisoned in 1840 on charges brought against him by his successor, General José Urrea. As far as can be determined, because Miracle's "Instructions" bear no date but do bear Filisola's name, the general must have

issued the orders before his dismissal; Urrea apparently allowed the orders to stand and sent Miracle out from Matamoros in 1838 to complete the mission.

60. Ibid.

61. "Companions and Friends" (1838?), S. Doc. 14, 13–14.

62. Diary of Julian Pedro Miracle, S. Doc. 14, 14–16.

63. Ibid., 16–17.

64. Ibid.; *Telegraph and Texas Register,* 29 September 1838.

65. John R. Wunder and Rebecca Herring, "Frontier Conspiracy: Law, History, Turner, and the Cordova Rebellion," *Red River Valley Historical Review* 7 (1982): 60–61.

66. Cordova to Flores, 19 July 1838, S. Doc. 14, 36; *Telegraph and Texas Register,* 29 September 1838.

67. *Telegraph and Texas Register,* 29 September 1838.

68. Houston to Rusk, 10 August 1838, AJHP, No. 1781.

68. Rusk Proclamation, 10 August 1838, Rusk Papers, Folder 2.

69. Houston to Mush, 10 August 1838, in Gulick, ed., *Lamar Papers* 2:198; Houston to Bowl, 11 August 1838, ibid.; Houston to Bowl, 12 August 1838, ibid., 2:201–2.

70. Houston to Many, 11 August 1838, AJHP, No. 1745.

71. Bowl to Houston, 11 August 1838, in Gulick, ed., *Lamar Papers* 2:200–1.

72. Ibid., Houston to Bowl, 12 August 1838, 2:201–2.

73. Houston to Rusk, 12 August 1838, Rusk Papers, Folder 2.

74. Houston to Rusk, 13 August 1838, Rusk Papers, Folder 2.

75. Rusk to Bowl, 13 August 1838, Rusk Papers, Folder 2; Rusk to Houston, 14 August 1838, AJHP, No. 1766; Bean letter captured with Miracle documents (1838?), NA.

76. Rusk to Houston, 14 August 1838, AJHP, No. 1768; Samuel Williams to Houston, 14 August 1838, AJHP, No. 1769.

77. Houston to Bowl, 14 August 1838, AJHP, No. 1767.

78. Rusk to Houston, 14 August 1838, AJHP, No. 1768; Samuel Williams to Houston, 14 August 1838, AJHP, No. 1769.

79. Rusk to Houston, 15 August 1838, AJHP, No. 1777.

80. Rusk to Bowl, 15 August 1838, Rusk to Houston, 16 August 1838, Rusk Papers, Folder 2.

81. J. M. Henrie to M. B. Lamar, 17 August 1838, in Gulick, ed., *Lamar Papers* 2:205.

82. General Order, 18 August 1838, in Gulick, ed., *Lamar Papers* 2:206; J. M. Henrie to M. B. Lamar, 17 August 1838, in Gulick, ed. *Lamar Papers* 2:205.

83. Rusk to Houston, 19 August 1838, AJHP, No. 1799; Bowl to Houston, 20 August 1838, AJHP, No. 1801.

84. Houston to Rusk, 26 August 1838, Rusk Papers, Folder 2.

85. Robert Irion to Anson Jones, 29 November 1838, in Garrison, ed., *Diplomatic Correspondence* 1:350–51.

86. Ibid.; Jones to Forsyth, 31 December 1838, S. Doc. 14, 11–12.

87. Rusk to Houston, 25 August 1838, AJHP, No. 1814; Houston to Many, 27 August 1838, AJHP, No. 1824; Rusk to Houston, 9 September 1838, AJHP, No. 1843; Thurston to Lamar, 14 September 1838, in Gulick, ed., *Lamar Papers,* 2:223–24; Rusk to Houston, 4 October 1838, AJHP, No. 1863.

88. Rusk to Houston, 4 October 1838, AJHP, No. 1863.

89. Rusk to Parker, 23 October 1838, in *Telegraph and Texas Register,* 9 November 1838.

90. Woldert, "Last of the Cherokees in Texas," 201–7; Rusk to Bowl, 9 October 1838, Rusk Papers, Folder 2.

91. McLeod to Lamar, 22 October 1838, in Gulick, ed., *Lamar Papers* 2:265–67.

92. Statement of Elias Vansickle, 23 January 1839, S. Doc. 14, 25.

93. Ibid.; Rusk to Parker, in *Telegraph and Texas Register,* 9 November 1838.

94. Rusk to Parker, *Telegraph and Texas Register,* 9 November 1838; McLeod to Lamar, 22 October 1838, in *Lamar Papers* 2:265–67.

95. Rusk to Bowl, 29 October 1838, *Lamar Papers,* 2:255.

96. Houston to Rusk, 10 October 1838, in Williams and Barker, eds., *Writings of Sam Houston* 2:288–89.

97. Bowl to Horton, 27 October 1838, in Gulick, ed., *Lamar Papers* 2:271.

98. A. Horton to Houston, 10 November 1838, in *Telegraph and Texas Register,* 28 November 1838.

5. "Between Two Fires": War and Removal, 1839–1840

1. Rusk to Douglass, 21 November 1838, Papers of James Harper Starr and Kelsey H. Douglass (Barker Texas History Center, University of Texas, Austin), Folder 4 (hereafter cited as Starr-Douglass Papers).

2. B. Waters to Douglass, 20 December 1838, Starr-Douglass Papers, Folder 4; Box to Douglass, 24 December 1838, Starr-Douglass Papers, Folder 4.

3. A. K. Christian, "Mirabeau Buonaparte Lamar," *Southwestern Historical Quarterly* 24 (1920): 72–79.

4. "Inaugural Address," in Gulick, ed., *Lamar Papers* 2:308; Muckleroy, "Indian Policy," 128–29.

5. Rusk to Douglass, 21 November 1838, Starr-Douglass Papers, Folder 4; Canalizo to Cordova, 27 February 1839 (translation), AJHP, No. 4602.19.

6. Canalizo, Passport to Flores, 9 March 1839 (translation), AJHP, No. 4602.19; Canalizo to Cordova, 1 March 1839 (translation), AJHP, No. 4602.19.

7. Canalizo to Flores, 27 February 1839 (translation), AJHP, No. 4602.19.

8. Ibid.

9. Ibid.

10. A. S. Johnston to Bowles, 10 April 1839, in Gulick, ed., *Lamar Papers* 2:522–23; *Telegraph and Texas Register,* 10 April 1839.

11. Burleson to Johnston, 22 May 1839, AJHP, No. 4602.19; Nance, *After San Jacinto,* 136–37. Flores's death was reported in this engagement, but the report may have been false. His survival was suggested in a story appearing in the *Texas Sentinel* on 11 March 1840, in which it was reported he had recently participated in a battle with Texan forces near the Rio Grande (see Nance, *After San Jacinto,* 240, for an account of this action). A few years later Manuel Flores and Vicente Cordova participated in the Mexican reinvasion of Texas led by General Adrian Woll in 1842, and both were commended by General Woll for gallantry. In his recommendation Woll noted that Cordova and Flores were "friends of the Caddo and Cherokee Indians" (Translation of Report from General Adrian Woll to Secretary of War and Navy, 20 September 1842, in General Miguel A. Sanchez Lamego, *The Second Mexican-Texas War, 1841–1843,* Hill Junior College Monograph No. 7, 106–7; William L. Mann, "James O. Rice, Hero of the Battle on the San Gabriels," *Southwestern Historical Quarterly* 55 (1955): 35–38.

12. Burleson to Johnston, 22 May 1839, AJHP, No. 4602.19.

13. A. S. Johnston to General Kelsey Douglass, 30 May 1839, Rusk Papers, Folder 3; Rusk to Houston, 9 June 1839, Rusk Papers, Folder 3; D. S. Kaufman to Houston, 18 June 1839, AJHP, No. 1945.

14. Bowl to Rusk, 26 May 1839, Rusk Papers, Folder 4.

15. Reagan, *Memoirs,* 30–31.

16. Lamar to Bowl, 26 May 1839, in Winfrey and Day, eds., *Texas Indian Papers* 1:64–65.

17. Reagan, *Memoirs,* 30–31.

18. Ibid.

19. Ibid. No such documentation is to be found in either the manuscript papers of John Ross (Gilcrease Institute, Tulsa) or in Gary E. Moulton's *The Papers of Chief John Ross,* 2 vols. (Norman: University of Oklahoma Press, 1985).

20. Lamar to Burnet, Johnston, Rusk, Burton, and Mayfield, 27 June 1839, in Winfrey and Day, eds., *Texas Indian Papers* 1:67–70.

21. Rusk, Burnet, Mayfield, Johnston, and Burton to Bolles [*sic*], 9 July 1839, Rusk Papers, Folder 3.

22. Ibid.

23. Mayfield's Journal, 8 July–19 July 1839, Rusk Papers, Folder 3.

24. Commissioners' Minutes, 11 July–15 July 1839, Rusk Papers, Folder 4.

25. Ibid.

26. Ibid.

27. Articles of Agreement, 14 July 1839, Rusk Papers, Folder 4. The term "removal" was used repeatedly throughout the commissioners' correspondence and field notes.

28. Commissioners' Minutes, Rusk Papers, Folder 4.

29. Ibid.

30. Ibid.

31. Mayfield's Report, 15 July 1839, Rusk Papers, Folder 4.

32. Ibid.

33. Ibid.

34. Ibid.

35. Duwali to David G. Burnet and other Commissioners, 14 July 1839, Rusk Papers, Folder 4.

36. Commissioners' Minutes, Rusk Papers, Folder 4.

37. Ibid.

38. Rusk to Douglass, 18 July 1839, Rusk Papers, Folder 3; Reagan, *Memoirs,* 32–34; "Report of General Kelsey H. Douglass of the engagement with Cherokees on the 15th July, 1839, to A. Sidney Johnston, Secretary of War," in Harriet Smither, ed., *Journals of the Fourth Congress of the Republic of Texas* 3:115–16.

39. Rusk to Douglass, 18 July 1839, Rusk Papers, Folder 3; Reagan, *Memoirs,* 34–35; Report of Douglass, in Smither, ed., *Journals of the Fourth Congress* 3:115–16.

40. Rusk to Douglass, 18 July 1839, Rusk Papers, Folder 2.

41. Rusk to Johnston, (?) September 1839, Rusk Papers, Folder 3.

42. Draft on Government, signed by Rusk, Mayfield, and Johnston, 1 August 1839, in Winfrey and Day, eds., *Texas Indian Papers* 1:80. In June 1839 the Texas government had set aside a total of $25,000 to compensate "the Cherokees and Associate Bands"; this fund had been established in a bank in Natchitoches, Louisiana, and the Indian commissioners were empowered to draw upon it for the necessary cash, supplies, and services (David Burnet to J. Reilly, 27 June 1839, in Winfrey and Day, eds., *Texas Indian Papers* 1:70). The money went unused due to the war of removal, and in early August $21,000 was returned to the Texas treasury. The remaining $4,000 was reserved for the use of the commissioners to deal with the Shawnees (ibid., Commissioners to J. Reilly, 1 August 1839, 1:78). The Texas government did follow through on its promise to compensate the Shawnees. On 2 August 1839 the Shawnees and the republic signed a treaty under which the Indians agreed to leave Texas, and the government agreed to pay them for their improvements and crops, furnish them supplies and transportation, and escort them from the country (ibid., "Treaty between Texas and the Shawnee Indians," 1:80–81). In September 1839 valuation of the Shawnees' property was completed, and sixty-three of them received a combined total of $7,806 from the Indian commissioners (ibid., "Valuation of Shawnee Property," 1:92–94). There is no evidence that Delawares, Kickapoos, or other of the "Associated Bands" received compensation.

43. Emberson to Johnston, 2 September 1839, AJHP, No. 4602.51.

44. Joseph W. Robertson to James S. Mayfield, 7 April 1841, in Winfrey and Day, eds., *Texas Indian Papers* 1:122.

45. *General-in-Chief of the Mexican Frontier to the Cherokees, Shawnees, Wacos, Kickapoos, Conchates, and other Indian Tribes,* 6 August 1840 (microfilm), E. de Golyer Library, Dallas, Texas.

46. Smith to Forsyth, 1 January 1840, U.S. Consular Papers, Roll 2, Matamoros; *Texas Sentinel,* 19 February 1840; *Texas Sentinel,* 18 March 1840; Bee to Forsyth, 15 December 1840, S. Doc. 14, 51; Bee to Forsyth, 23 January 1841, S. Doc. 14, 55.

47. Arbuckle to Joseph Vann, 9 October 1840, Cherokee Agency West, Roll 84, frame 0247; Joseph W. Robertson to James S. Mayfield, 7 April 1841, in Winfrey and Day, eds., *Texas Indian Papers* 1:122; Carolyn Foreman, "Texanna," *Chronicles of Oklahoma* 31 (1953): 178; Anna Lewis, "Trading Post at the Crossing of the Chickasaw Trails," *Chronicles of Oklahoma* 12 (1934): 448.

48. Arbuckle to Joseph Vann, 23 May 1840, Cherokee Agency West, Roll 84, frame 0202.

49. William G. McLoughlin's *Cherokee Renascence* (1986) provides a detailed analysis of the nationalistic revival between 1794 and 1833 that resulted in a revitalized Cherokee nation.

50. Starr, *Early History of the Cherokees;* Strickland, *Fire and the Spirits,* 68.

51. Captain John Stuart, *A Sketch of the Cherokee and Choctaw Indians,* 7–14.

52. Ibid., 14, 17.

53. Ibid., 18–20.

54. Ibid., 16.

55. Ibid., 16–17.

56. Kappler, comp., *Indian Affairs* 2:288–92.

57. Mooney, *Myths,* 142–43; Markman, "The Arkansas Cherokees," 183–92; Wardell, *Political History of the Cherokee Nation,* 6–8.

58. Woodward, *Cherokees,* 208–9; Russell Thornton, "Cherokee Population Losses During the Trail of Tears: A New Perspective and a New Estimate, *Ethnohistory* 31 (1984): 298–300. On 29 December 1835 representatives of the Cherokee nation signed the Treaty of New Echota, by which the nation ceded its lands east of the Mississippi for compensations including $5 million, additional land in the West, and transportation westward. Although the treaty was opposed by a large portion of the nation, a deadline for removal was set for 23 May 1838. During the intervening years between 1835 and 1838, several thousand supporters of the Treaty of New Echota emigrated westward.

59. Arbuckle to Joseph Vann, 23 May 1840, Cherokee Agency West, Roll 84, frame 0202; Arbuckle to Poinsett, 27 May 1840, Cherokee Agency West, Roll 84, frame 0210; Foreman, "Dutch," 255–58, 264.

60. Chiefs to Arbuckle, 3 June 1840, Cherokee Agency West, Roll 84, frame 0125.

61. Arbuckle to Joseph Vann, 9 October 1840, Cherokee Agency West, Roll 84, frame 0247.

62. Ibid.

63. Major William Armstrong to Hartley Crawford, 20 August 1839, Cherokee Agency West, Roll 83, frame 0047.

64. Emberson to Johnston, 2 September 1839, AHJP, No. 4602.19.

65. Arbuckle to Lamar, 28 April 1840, in Garrison, ed., *Diplomatic Correspondence* 1:455; Archer to Arbuckle, 11 June 1840, ibid.; *Texas Sentinel,* 13 June 1840; Receipt for Hauling Cherokee Prisoners, 5 May 1840, Receipt for

Beef for Cherokee Prisoners, 15 June 1840, Republic of Texas Collection.

66. Arbuckle to Joseph Vann, 9 October 1840, Cherokee Agency West, Roll 84, frame 0247.

67. George Kendall, *Narrative of the Texan-Santa Fe Expedition* 1:106; *Texas Sentinel*, 18 March 1840.

68. Almonte to John Brown, 20 June 1840, S. Doc. 14, 54.

69. *Cherokee Advocate*, 26 June 1845; Grant Foreman, "The Story of Sequoyah's Last Days," *Chronicles of Oklahoma* 12 (1934): 255–341.

70. Woll's Report, in Lamego, *The Second Mexican-Texas War*, 30; "Diary of Adolphus Sterne," ed. Harriet Smither, *Southwestern Historical Quarterly* 31 (1931): 262.

71. Treaty of Bird's Fort, September 29, 1843, in Winfrey and Day, eds., *Texas Indian Papers* 1:241–46; Muckleroy, "Indian Policy," 188–91.

72. Ledger Sheet of Gifts to Indians, in Winfrey and Day, eds., *Texas Indian Papers* 1:281.

73. Muckleroy, "Indian Policy," 193–96.

74. Ibid., 197–99.

75. Foreman, "Sequoyah's Last Days," 337–41.

76. Arbuckle to Adjutant General, 29 November 1845, Grant Foreman Papers, 36–76; *Arkansas Intelligencer*, 10 January 1846; interview with W. W. Harnage, n.d., Indian-Pioneer Papers, 4:334–37.

77. Treaty Party to General Arbuckle, 15 November 1845, H. Doc. 92, 29th Cong., 1st sess., 1846, 23; Arbuckle to Adjutant General, 13 January 1846; S. Doc. 301, 29th Cong., 1st sess., 1846, 6; Lee David Benton, "An Odyssey into Texas: William Quesenbury with the Cherokees," *Chronicles of Oklahoma* 60 (1982): 125; *Arkansas Intelligencer*, 10 January 1846; Memorial of Cherokee Chiefs, on behalf of Old Settlers west of the Mississippi, H. Exec. Doc. 235, 28th Cong., 1st sess., 1844, 21–35.

78. Wardell, *Political History of the Cherokee Nation*, 59–60; Woodward, *Cherokees*, 235–36.

79. Woodward, *Cherokees*, 236–37; Wardell, *Political History of the Cherokee Nation*, 66–75.

80. Woodward, *Cherokees*, 235.

Epilogue

1. Wardell, *Political History of the Cherokee Nation*, 123–39; Woodward, *Cherokees*, 255–69.

2. Interview with W. W. Harnage (undated), Indian-Pioneer Papers; Nancy Starr to Sarah Watie, 24 July 1854, in Edward Everett Dale and Gaston Litton, eds., *Cherokee Cavaliers: Forty Years of Cherokee History as Told in the Correspondence of the Ridge-Watie-Boudinot Families*, 79; Sarah Watie to Stand Watie, 20 May 1863, ibid.; Sarah Watie to Stand Watie, 28 July 1863, ibid.; Wardell, *Political History of the Cherokee Nation*, 163–64.

3. James L. Butler to Stand Watie, 13 July 1865, in Dale and Litton, eds., *Cherokee Cavaliers*, 235; Richard Fields et. al., to Honorable Commis-

sioners, 20 September 1865, ibid., 237; Thomas F. Anderson to Stand Watie, 19 February 1866, ibid., 240.

4. Petition, 10 October 1866, Laws of the Cherokee Nation, 1866, Cherokee National Records.

5. "History of Suit Filed by Texas Cherokees" (transcript), Indian-Pioneer Papers, 18:357–59.

6. Agreement between W. P. Adair and John C. Frémont, 6 February 1871, Israel G. Vore Papers; Israel Vore to General J. W. Denver, 24 July 1882, "Texas Cherokees," (transcript), Vore Papers; Vore to Denver, 8 January 1883, Vore Papers.

7. "History of Suit Filed by Texas Cherokees," Indian-Pioneer Papers, 18:357–58; Clarke, *Texas Cherokees,* 120–21.

8. "Invoices, Cherokee Indians," General Land Office of Texas, Records and Archives Division, Austin, Texas.

9. Clarke, *Texas Cherokees,* 122–23.

10. *Daily Oklahoman,* 26 July 1963; Clarke, *Texas Cherokees,* 124–25.

Bibliography

Primary Materials

Documents

Archivo General de México. Secretaria de Fomento-Colonización. Transcripts. Archives, Texas State Library. Austin, Texas.
Bexar Archives. Austin: University of Texas Library Microfilm Publications, 1970.
Cherokee National Records. Oklahoma Historical Society. Oklahoma City, Oklahoma.
General-in-Chief of the Mexican Frontier to the Cherokees, Shawnees, Wacos, Kickapoos, Conchates, and other Indian Tribes. Microfilm. E. de Golyer Library. Dallas, Texas.
Foreman, Grant. Papers. Manuscript Collections, Thomas Gilcrease Institute of American History and Art. Tulsa, Oklahoma.
Houston, Andrew Jackson. Papers. Archives, Texas State Library. Austin, Texas.
Indian-Pioneer Papers. Archives, Oklahoma Historical Society. Oklahoma City, Oklahoma.
Jackson, Andrew, Papers. Presidential Papers Series. Microfilm. Washington, D.C.: National Archives and Records Service, 1961.
Nacogdoches Archives. Archives, Texas State Library. Austin, Texas.
Records of the Bureau of Indian Affairs. Letterbook of the Arkansas Trading

House. Microfilm M-142. Washington, D.C.: National Archives and Records Service, 1948.

———. Letterbook of the Natchitoches–Sulphur Fork Factory, 1809–1821. Microfilm T-1029. Washington, D.C.: National Archives and Records Service, 1968.

———. Letters Received by the Office of Indian Affairs, 1824–1881. Cherokee Agency West, 1824–1836. Microfilm M-234. Washington, D.C.: National Archives and Records Service, 1959.

———. Records of the Cherokee Indian Agency in Tennessee, 1801–1835. Microfilm M-208. Washington, D.C.: National Archives Microfilm Publications, 1952.

———. Records of the Secretary of War Relating to Indian Affairs. Letters Received, 1800–1823. Microfilm M-271. Washington, D.C.: National Archives and Records Service, 1959.

———. Records of the Secretary of War Relating to Indian Affairs. Letters Sent, 1800–1824. Microfilm M-15. Washington, D.C.: National Archives Microfilm Publications, 1942.

Records of U.S. Army Continental Commands, 1821–1920. Record Group 393. Fort Gibson Letterbook. National Archives. Washington, D.C.

Republic of Texas Collection. Library. Special Collections. University of Texas at Arlington. Arlington, Texas.

Ross, John. Papers. Thomas Gilcrease Institute of American History and Art. Manuscripts Collection. Tulsa, Oklahoma.

Rusk, Thomas Jefferson. Papers. Eugene C. Barker Texas History Collection. University of Texas. Austin, Texas.

Saltillo Archives. Transcripts. Eugene C. Barker Texas History Collection. University of Texas. Austin, Texas.

Spanish Archives. Appendix to Translations of Empresario Contracts. General Land Office. Austin, Texas.

———. Record of Translations of Empresario Contracts. General Land Office. Austin, Texas.

Starr, James Harper. Papers (includes Papers of Kelsey H. Douglass). Eugene C. Barker Texas History Collection. University of Texas. Austin, Texas.

Texas. Department of State. Records Relating to Indian Affairs, 1825–1890. Archives, Texas State Library. Austin, Texas.

U.S. Congress. House of Representatives. Executive Document 351, 25th Cong. 2d sess., 1838.

———. Executive Document 235. 28th Cong., 1st sess., 1844.

———. Executive Document 92. 29th Cong., 1st sess., 1846.

U.S. Congress. Senate. Executive Document 301. 29th Cong., 1st sess., 1846.

———. Executive Document 14. 32d Cong., 2d sess., 1853.

U.S. Department of State. Consular Despatches. Matamoros. Microfilm M 281. Washington, D.C.: National Archives and Records Service, 1954.

Vore, Israel G. Papers. Oklahoma Historical Society. Oklahoma City, Oklahoma.

Newspapers

Arkansas Gazette (Arkansas Post, Missouri Territory), 1818–1820.
Arkansas Intelligencer (Little Rock, Arkansas), 10 January 1846.
Cherokee Advocate (Tahlequah, Cherokee Nation), 26 June 1845.
Daily Oklahoman (Oklahoma City, Oklahoma), 1963.
Knoxville Gazette (Knoxville, Tennessee), 1791–1818.
National Intelligencer (Washington, D.C.). 1820.
Niles Weekly Register (Baltimore, Maryland). 1812–1820.
Telegraph and Texas Register (Houston, Texas). 1835.
Texas Gazette (San Felipe de Austin, Texas), 3 July 1830.
Texas Sentinel (Austin, Texas), 1840–1841.

Published Primary Works

Abstract of All Original Texas Land Titles Comprising Grants and Locations to August 31, 1941. Austin, Texas: General Land Office, 1941.

Almonte, Juan N. *Noticia Estadística Sobre Tejas.* Mexico: Ignacio Cumplido, 1835; facsimile edition, *Northern Mexico on the Eve of the United States Invasion: Rare Imprints Concerning California, Arizona, New Mexico, and Texas, 1821–1846.* Edited by David J. Weber. New York: Arno Press, 1976.

———. "Statistical Report on Texas." Edited by Carlos Castañeda. *Southwestern Historical Quarterly* 28 (January, 1925): 177–222.

American State Papers. Documents, Legislative and Executive, of the Congress of the United States. 38 vols. Washington, D.C.: Gales and Seaton, 1834.

Berlandier, Jean Louis. *The Indians of Texas in 1830.* Edited by John C. Ewers. Translated by Patricia R. Leclercq. Washington, D.C.: Smithsonian Institution Press, 1969.

Barker, Eugene C., ed. *The Austin Papers. Annual Report of the American Historical Association for the Year 1922.* 2 vols and supplement. Washington, D.C. GPO, 1928.

Barker, Eugene C., ed. "Journal of the Permanent Council, October 11 to 27, 1835." *Southwestern Historical Quarterly* 7 (April 1904): 249–78.

Bartram, William. *Travels Through North and South Carolina, Georgia, East and West Florida.* Philadelphia: James and Johnson, 1791.

Carter, Clarence E., ed. and comp. *Territorial Papers of the United States.* 26 vols. Washington, D.C.: GPO, 1934–1962.

Dale, Edward Everett, and Gaston Litton, eds. *Cherokee Cavaliers: Forty Years of Cherokee History as Told in the Correspondence of the Ridge-Watie-Boudinot Family.* Norman, Okla.: University of Oklahoma Press, 1939.

Gammel, H. P. N. *The Laws of Texas, 1822–1897.* Austin, Texas: Gammel Book Co., 1898.

Garrison, George P., ed. *Diplomatic Correspondence of the Republic of Texas.* 3 vols. Washington, D.C.: GPO, 1908.
Green, Rena Maverick, ed. *Sam Maverick, Texas: A Collection of Letters, etc.* San Antonio, Texas: privately printed, 1952.
Gulick, Charles A., Jr., Winnie Allen, Katherine Elliott, and Harriet Smither. *The Papers of Mirabeau Buonaparte Lamar.* 6 vols. Austin, Texas: Pemberton Press, 1968.
Hodge, F. W., and Theodore H. Lewis, eds. *Spanish Explorers in the Southern United States, 1528–1543.* New York: Charles Schribner's Sons, 1907; facsimile edition, Austin, Texas: Texas State Historical Association, 1984.
Houck, Louis, ed. *The Spanish Regime in Missouri.* 2 vols. Chicago, Ill.: R. R. Donnelley and Sons, 1909.
Jackson, Donald, ed. *Letters of the Lewis and Clark Expedition, 1783–1854.* Urbana, Ill.: University of Illinois Press, 1962.
Jenkins, John H., ed. *Papers of the Texas Revolution, 1835–1836.* 10 vols. Austin, Texas: Presidial Press, 1973.
Kappler, Charles J., comp. *Indian Affairs: Laws and Treaties.* 5 vols. Washington, D.C.: GPO, 1904–41.
Kendall, George W. *Narrative of the Texas Santa Fe Expedition.* 2 vols. London, England: Putnam and Wiley, 1844; reprint ed., Austin, Texas: Steck, 1935.
Kinnaird, Lawrence. *Spain in the Mississippi Valley, 1765–1794: Translations of Materials from the Spanish Archives in the Bancroft Library.* 3 vols. Annual Report of the American Historical Association for 1945. Washington, D.C.: GPO, 1946.
Laws of the Cherokee Nation Adopted by the Council at Various Periods. Tahlequah, Cherokee Nation, Indian Territory: Cherokee Advocate Office, 1852; reprint ed., Wilmington, Del.: Scholarly Resources, Inc., 1973.
Malloy, William M. *Treaties, Conventions, International Acts, Protocols, and Agreements Between the United States of America and Other Powers, 1776–1937.* 4 vols. Washington, D.C.: GPO, 1910–1938.
Mooney, James G. *The Sacred Formulas of the Cherokees. Seventh Annual Report of the Bureau of American Ethnology, 1885–1886.* Washington, D.C.: GPO, 1891.
Mooney, James G., and Frans M. Olbrechts. *The Swimmer Manuscript: Cherokee Sacred Formulas and Medicinal Prescriptions.* Bulletin 99, Bureau of American Ethnology. Washington, D.C.: GPO, 1932.
Morse, Jedidiah. *A Report to the Secretary of War of the United States, on Indian Affairs. Comprising a Narrative of a Tour Performed in the Summer of 1820, under a Commission from the President of the United States. . . .* New Haven, Connecticut: Howe and Spalding, 1822.
Padilla, Juan Antonio. "Report on the Barbarous Indians of the Province of Texas." Translated by Mattie Austin Hatcher. *Southwestern Historical Quarterly* 23 (July 1919), 47–60.
Reagan, John Hunter. *Memoirs.* Edited by Walter F. McCaleb. New York: Neal Publishing Co., 1906.

Ridge, John. "The Cherokee War Path." Edited by Carolyn T. Foreman. *Chronicles of Oklahoma* 9 (September 1931): 233–63.

Ruíz, Jose Francisco. *Report on the Indian Tribes of Texas in 1828.* Edited by John C. Ewers. Translated by Georgette Dorn. New Haven, Connecticut: Yale University Library, 1972.

Sibley, Dr. John. *A Report from Natchitoches in 1807.* Edited by Frederick W. Hodge. Indian Notes and Monographs Series. New York: Heye Foundation, 1922.

Sánchez, José María. "A Trip to Texas in 1828." Translated by Carlos Castañeda. *Southwestern Historical Quarterly* 29 (April 1926): 249–88.

Smither, Harriet, ed. "Diary of Adolphus Sterne," *Southwestern Historical Quarterly* 31 (January 1931): 262–69.

———. *Journals of the Fourth Congress of the Republic of Texas.* 3 vols. Austin, Texas: Von Boeckmann-Jones Co., 1931.

Stuart, Captain John. *A Sketch of the Cherokee and Choctaw Nations.* Little Rock, Arkansas: Woodruff and Pew, 1837.

Taylor, Virginia H., ed. *The Letters of Antonio Martínez, Last Spanish Governor of Texas, 1817–1822.* Translated by Virginia H. Taylor. Austin, Texas: Texas State Library, 1957.

Thwaites, Reuben Gold, ed. *Early Western Travels.* 32 vols. Cleveland, Ohio: Arthur H. Clark Co., 1904–1907. Vol. 3. Edwin James, *Account of an Expedition from Pittsburgh to the Rocky Mountains, Performed in the Years 1819 and 1820.*

———. *Early Western Travels.* 32 vols. Cleveland, Ohio: Arthur H. Clark Co., 1904–1907. Vol. 13, Thomas Nuttall, *Journal of Travels into the Arkansas Territory, October 2, 1818–February 18, 1820.*

———. *Original Journals of the Lewis and Clark Expedition.* Milwaukee: State Historical Society of Wisconsin, 1905; reprint ed., New York: Arno Press, 1969.

Walker, Henry P., ed. "William McLane's Narrative of the Magee-Gutiérrez Expedition, 1812–1813." *Southwestern Historical Quarterly* 46 (January 1942), 569–88.

Washburn, Cephas. *Reminiscences of the Indians.* Edited by Rev. J. W. Moore. Richmond, Va.: Presbyterian Committee of Publication, 1869.

Williams, Amelia W., and Eugene C. Barker, eds. *The Writings of Sam Houston, 1813–1863.* 3 vols. Austin, Texas: University of Texas Press, 1938.

Winfrey, Dorman, and James M. Day. *The Texas Indian Papers, 1825–1843.* 4 vols. Austin, Texas: Texas State Library, 1959.

Winkler, Ernest W., ed. *Secret Journals of the Senate of the Republic of Texas, 1836–1845.* Austin, Texas: Austin Printing Co., 1911.

Maps

Map of Texas, Compiled from a Survey Recorded in the Land Office of Texas, and Other Official Surveys. 1841. General Land Office. Austin, Texas.

Secondary Materials

Books

Amsden, Charles Avery. *Navajo Weaving: Its Technic and Its History.* Santa Ana, Calif.: Fine Arts Press, 1934.

Barnes, Thomas C., Thomas H. Naylor, and Charles W. Polzer. *Northern New Spain: A Research Guide.* Tucson, Ariz.: University of Arizona Press, 1981.

Binkley, William C. *The Texas Revolution.* Baton Rouge, La.: Louisiana State University Press, 1952; reprint ed., Austin, Texas: Texas State Historical Association, 1979.

Brown, John Henry. *History of Texas from 1685 to 1892.* St. Louis, Mo.: L. E. Daniell, 1893.

Clarke, Mary Whatley. *Chief Bowles and the Texas Cherokees.* Civilization of the American Indian Series, No. 113. Norman, Okla.: University of Oklahoma Press, 1971.

Corkran, David H. *The Cherokee Frontier: Conflict and Survival, 1740–1762.* Norman, Okla.: University of Oklahoma Press, 1962.

Dale, Edward Everett, and Gaston Litton, eds. *Cherokee Cavaliers: Forty Years of Cherokee History as Told in the Correspondence of the Ridge-Watie-Boudinot Family.* Norman, Okla.: University of Oklahoma Press, 1939.

De Shields, James T. *Cynthia Ann Parker: The Story of Her Capture at the Massacre of the Inmates of Parker's Fort.* St. Louis, Mo.: privately published, 1886.

Dickens, Roy S. *Cherokee Prehistory: The Pisgah Phase in the Appalachian Summit Region.* Knoxville, Tenn.: University of Tennessee Press, 1976.

Drinnon, Richard. *White Savage: The Case of John Dunn Hunter.* New York: Schocken Books, 1972.

Fenton, William N., and John Gulick, eds. *Symposium on Cherokee and Iroquois Culture.* Bulletin 180, Bureau of American Ethnology. Washington, D.C.: GPO, 1961.

Finger, John R. *The Eastern Band of Cherokees, 1819–1900.* Knoxville, Tenn.: University of Tennessee Press, 1984.

Fogelson, Raymond D. *The Cherokees: A Critical Bibliography.* Bloomington, Ind.: Indiana University Press, 1978.

Foote, Henry S. *Texas and the Texans.* Philadelphia, Penn.: Thomas, Cowperthwait, and Co., 1841.

Foreman, Grant. *Indians and Pioneers: The Story of the American Southwest before 1830.* Civilization of the American Indian Series, No. 14. Norman, Okla.: University of Oklahoma Press, 1936.

Fried, Morton H. *The Evolution of Political Society: An Essay in Political Anthropology.* New York: Random House, 1967.

Friend, Llerena. *Sam Houston, The Great Designer.* Austin, Texas: University of Texas Press, 1954; Texas History Paperback, 1969.

Gearing, Frederick O. *Priests and Warriors: Social Structures for Cherokee Politics in the 18th Century.* American Anthropological Association memoir No. 93. Menasha, Wis.: American Anthropological Association, 1962.
Gilbert, William H. *The Eastern Cherokees.* Bulletin 133, Bureau of American Ethnology. Washington, D.C.: GPO, 1943.
Goodwin, Gary C. *Cherokees in Transition: A Study of Changing Culture and Environment Prior to 1775.* University of Chicago Department of Geography Research Paper No. 181. Chicago, Ill.: University of Chicago, 1977.
Gregory, Jack, and Rennard Strickland. *Sam Houston with the Cherokees 1829–1833.* Austin, Texas: University of Texas Press, 1967.
Hatcher, Mattie Austin. *The Opening of Texas to Foreign Settlement, 1801–1821.* Austin, Texas: University of Texas Press, 1927.
Hudson, Charles M., ed. *The Southeastern Indians.* Knoxville, Tenn.: University of Tennessee Press, 1976.
John, Elizabeth A. H. *Storms Brewed in Other Men's Worlds: The Confrontation of Indians, Spanish, and French in the Southwest, 1540–1794.* College Station, Texas: Texas A & M University Press, 1975.
Kilpatrick, Jack, and Rennard Strickland. *Sam Houston with the Cherokees, 1829–1833.* Austin, Texas: University of Texas Press, 1967.
King, Duane H., ed. *The Cherokee Indian Nation: A Troubled History.* Knoxville, Tenn.: University of Tennessee Press, 1979.
Krieger, Alex D. *Culture Complexes and Chronology in Northern Texas.* University of Texas Publication No. 4640. Austin, Texas: University of Texas Press, 1947.
Lamego, General Miguel A. Sanchez. *The Second Mexican-Texas War, 1841–1843.* Hill Junior College Monograph No. 7. Hillsboro, Texas: Hill Junior College, 1972.
Lowie, Robert H. *Indians of the Plains.* New York: McGraw-Hill Book Co., Inc., 1954; reprint ed., Garden City, N.Y.: Natural History Press, 1963.
Malone, Henry T. *Cherokees of the Old South: A People in Transition.* Athens, Ga.: University of Georgia Press, 1956.
Marshall, Thomas M. *A History of the Western Boundary of the Louisiana Purchase, 1819–1841.* Berkeley, Calif.: University of California Press, 1914; reprint ed., New York: Da Capo Press, 1970.
Matthews, John Joseph. *The Osages: Children of the Middle Waters.* Civilization of the American Indian Series, No. 60. Norman, Okla.: University of Oklahoma Press, 1961.
McLoughlin, William G. *Cherokee Renascence in the New Republic.* Princeton, N.J.: Princeton University Press, 1986.
———. *Cherokees and Missionaries, 1789–1839.* New Haven, Conn.: Yale University Press, 1984.
Miller, Thomas F. *The Public Lands of Texas, 1519–1970.* Norman, Okla.: University of Oklahoma Press, 1972.
Mooney, James G. *Myths of the Cherokees. Nineteenth Annual Report of the*

Bureau of American Ethnology, 1897–1898. Washington, D.C.: GPO, 1900.
Nance, Joseph M. *After San Jacinto: The Texas-Mexican Frontier, 1836–1841.* Austin, Texas: University of Texas Press, 1963.
———. *Attack and Counter-Attack: The Texas-Mexican Frontier, 1842.* Austin, Texas: University of Texas Press, 1964.
Nash, Manning. *Primitive and Peasant Economic Systems.* San Francisco: Chandler Publishing Co., 1966.
Newcomb, William W. *The Indians of Texas.* Austin, Texas: University of Texas Press, 1961.
Parkes, Henry Bamford. *A History of Mexico.* New York: Houghton Mifflin Co., 1969.
Perdue, Theda. *Slavery and the Evolution of Cherokee Society.* Knoxville, Tenn.: University of Tennessee Press, 1979.
Redfield, Robert. *The Little Community: Viewpoints for the Study of a Human Whole.* Chicago, Ill.: University of Chicago Press, 1956.
Reid, John Phillip. *A Better Kind of Hatchet: Law, Trade, and Diplomacy in the Cherokee Nation During the Early Years of European Contact.* University Park, Pa.: University of Pennsylvania Press, 1976.
———. *A Law of Blood: The Primitive Law of the Cherokee Nation.* New York: New York University Press, 1970.
Royce, Charles C. *The Cherokee Nation of Indians.* Fifth Annual Report of the Bureau of American Ethnology, 1883–1884. Washington, D.C.: GPO, 1887.
Sahlins, Marshall D. *Tribesmen.* Englewood Cliffs, N.J.: Prentice-Hall, Inc., 1968.
Serrano y Saenz, Manuel. *España y los Indios Cherakis y Chactas en la Segunda Mitad del Siglo XVIII.* Seville, Spain: Tipo de la "Guia Official," 1916.
Service, Elman R. *Primitive Social Organization: An Evolutionary Perspective.* New York: Random House, 1962.
Skinner, S. A. *Historical Archeology of the Neches Saline in Smith County, Texas.* THSC Archeological Report No. 21. Austin, Texas: THSC, 197.
Starkey, Marion. *The Cherokee Nation.* New York, New York: Alfred A. Knopf, 1946.
Starr, Emmet. *Early History of the Cherokees: Embracing Aboriginal Customs, Religion, Laws, Folklore, and Civilization.* Claremore, Okla.: privately published, 1917.
———. *History of the Cherokee Indians and their Legends and Folklore.* Oklahoma City, Oklahoma: privately published, 1938; reprint ed., New York: Kraus, 1969.
Strickland, Rennard. *Fire and the Spirits: Cherokee Law from Clan to Court.* Norman, Okla.: University of Oklahoma Press, 1975.
Suhm, Dee Ann, Alex D. Krieger, and Edward B. Jelks. *An Introductory Handbook of Texas Archeology.* Bulletin 25 of the Texas Archeological Society. Austin, Texas. TAS, 1954.
Swanton, John R. *Source Material on the History and Ethnology of the*

Caddo Indians. Bulletin 132, Bureau of American Ethnology. Washington, D.C.: GPO, 1942.

———. *The Indians of the Southeastern United States.* Bulletin 137, Bureau of American Ethnology. Washington, D.C.: GPO, 1946.

Vigness, David M. *The Revolutionary Decades.* Austin, Texas: Steck-Vaughan, 1965.

Wallace, Ernest F., and E. Adamson Hoebel. *The Comanches: Lords of the South Plains.* Civilization of the American Indian Series, No. 34. Norman, Okla.: University of Oklahoma Press, 1952.

Wardell, Morris. *A Political History of the Cherokee Nation, 1838–1907.* Civilization of the American Indian Series, No. 17. Norman, Okla.: University of Oklahoma Press, 1939, 1977.

Webb, William S. *An Archeological Survey of the Norris Basin in Eastern Tennessee.* Bulletin 118, Bureau of American Ethnology. Washington, D.C.: GPO, 1938.

Woldert, Albert. *History of Tyler and Smith County, Texas.* San Antonio, Texas: Naylor Co., 1948.

Woodward, Grace Steele. *The Cherokees.* Civilization of the American Indian Series, No. 65. Norman, Okla.: University of Oklahoma Press, 1963.

Yoakum, Henderson. *History of Texas, from Its First Settlement in 1685 to Its Annexation to the United States in 1846.* 2 vols. New York: J. S. Redfield, 1855.

Articles

Barker, Eugene C. "The Battle of Velasco." *Southwestern Historical Quarterly* 7 (1903): 326–28.

Bates, W. B. "A Sketch History of Nacogdoches." *Southwestern Historical Quarterly* 49 (April 1946): 491–97.

Benton, Lee David. "An Odyssey into Texas: William Quesenbury with the Cherokees." *Chronicles of Oklahoma* 60 (Summer 1982), 116–135.

Berry, Jane M. "The Indian Policy of Spain in the Southwest, 1783–1795." *Mississippi Valley Historical Review* 3 (March 1917): 462–77.

Bloom, Leonard. "The Acculturation of the Eastern Cherokee: Historical Aspects." *North Carolina Historical Review* 19 (October 1942): 323–58.

———. "The Cherokee Clan: A Study in Acculturation." *American Anthropologist* 41 (April 1939): 266–268.

Bugbee, Lester G. "The Texas Frontier, 1820–1825." *Proceedings of the Southern Historical Association* 4 (1929): 102–21.

Corkran, David. "Cherokee Pre-History." *North Carolina Historical Review* 34 (October 1957): 455–66.

Christian, A. K. "Mirabeau Buonaparte Lamar." *Southwestern Historical Quarterly* 24 (July 1920): 39–80.

Cox, Isaac J. "Explorations of the Louisiana Frontier, 1803–1805." *Annual Report of the American Historical Association for 1904,* pp. 149–74. Washington, D.C.: GPO, 1905.

Davis, E. M. "The Caddoan Area." *Bulletin of the Texas Archeological Society* 31 (1960): 77–143.

Dickens, Roy S. "The Origins and Development of Cherokee Culture." In *The Cherokee Indian Nation: A Troubled History,* edited by Duane King. Knoxville, Tenn.: University of Tennessee Press, 1979.

Faulk, Odie B. "The Penetration of Foreigners and Foreign Ideas into Spanish East Texas." *East Texas Historical Journal* 2 (1964): 87–96.

Fenton, William N. "Factionalism in American Indian Society." *Papers of the Fourth International Congress of Anthropological and Ethnological Science.* Vienna, Austria: n.p., 1952.

Fogelson, Raymond D., and Paul Kutsche. "Cherokee Economic Cooperatives: The Gadugh." In *Symposium on Cherokee and Iroquois Culture,* edited by William N. Fenton and John Gulick. Bulletin 180, Bureau of American Ethnology. Washington, D.C.: GPO, 1961.

Foreman, Carolyn T. "Dutch." *Chronicles of Oklahoma* 27 (Autumn 1949): 252–67.

———. "Texanna." *Chronicles of Oklahoma* 31 (Summer 1953): 178–88.

Foreman, Grant, ed. "The Story of Sequoyah's Last Days." *Chronicles of Oklahoma* 12 (March 1934): 255–41.

Garrett, Julia K., ed. "Doctor John Sibley and the Louisiana-Texas Frontier, 1804–1814." *Southwestern Historical Quarterly* 49 (April 1946): 599–614.

Gearing, Frederick O. "The Structural Poses of 18th Century Cherokee Villages." *American Anthropologist* 60 (December 1958): 1148–57.

Haggard, J. Villasana. "The Neutral Ground Between Louisiana and Texas." *Louisiana Historical Quarterly* 28 (October 1945): 1001–128.

Harper, Elizabeth. "The Taovayas Indians in Frontier Trade and Diplomacy, 1779–1835." *Panhandle-Plains Historical Review* 26 (1953): 41–72.

Harris, Helen Willits. "Almonte's Inspection of Texas in 1834." *Southwestern Historical Quarterly* 41 (January 1938): 135–211.

Hatcher, Mattie Austin. "The Louisiana Background of the Colonization of Texas, 1763–1803." *Southwestern Historical Quarterly* 24 (January 1921): 168–94.

Henderson, Harry M. "The Magee-Gutiérrez Expedition." *Southwestern Historical Quarterly* 55 (July 1951): 43–61.

Henderson, Mary Virginia. "Minor Empresario Contracts for the Colonization of Texas, 1825–1835." *Southwestern Historical Quarterly* 31 (April 1928): 295–324; 32 (July 1928): 1–28.

Houren, Alleine. "The Causes and Origin of the Decree of April 6, 1830." *Southwestern Historical Quarterly* 16 (1913): 378–442.

Jones, Robert L., and Pauline Jones. "The Occupation of Nacogdoches." *East Texas Historical Journal* 11 (1973): 23–43.

Lewis, Anna. "Trading Post at the Crossing of the Chickasaw Trails." *Chronicles of Oklahoma* 12 (December 1934): 447–53.

McClendon, R. Earl. "The First Treaty of the Republic of Texas." *Southwestern Historical Quarterly* 52 (July 1948): 32–48.

McLoughlin, William G. "Thomas Jefferson and the Beginning of Cherokee

Nationalism, 1806–1809." *William and Mary Quarterly* 32 (October 1975): 547–80.

Mann, William L. "James O. Rice, Hero of the Battle of the San Gabriels." *Southwestern Historical Quarterly* 55 (July 1955): 30–42.

Miller, Walter B. "Two Concepts of Authority." *American Anthropologist* 57 (April 1955): 271–89.

Morton, Ohland. "Life of General Don Manuel Mier y Terán, as It Affected Texas-Mexican Relations." *Southwestern Historical Quarterly* 47 (October 1943): 120–42.

Muckleroy, Anna. "The Indian Policy of the Republic of Texas." *Southwestern Historical Quarterly* 25 (April 1922): 229–60; 26 (July 1922): 1–29; 26 (October 1922): 128–48; 26 (January 1923): 184–206.

Parsons, Edmund M. "The Fredonian Rebellion." *Texana* 21 (Spring 1967): 11–52.

Persico, Richard V. "Cherokee Political Organization." In *The Cherokee Nation: A Troubled History,* edited by Duane King. Knoxville, Tenn.: University of Tennessee Press, 1979.

Perdue, Theda. "People Without a Place: Aboriginal Cherokee Bondage." *Indian Historian* 9 (Summer 1976): 31–37.

Reagan, John H. "The Expulsion of the Cherokees from East Texas." *Quarterly of the Texas State Historical Association* 1 (1897): 38–46.

Reid, John Phillip. "A Perilous Rule: The Law of International Homicide." In *The Cherokee Indian Nation: A Troubled History,* edited by Duane King. Knoxville, Tenn.: University of Tennessee Press, 1976.

Rowe, Edna. "The Disturbance at Anahuac in 1832." *Southwestern Historical Quarterly* 6 (April 1903): 265–99.

Setzler, Frank M., and Jesse D. Jennings. "Peachtree Mound and Village Site, Cherokee County, North Carolina." In Bulletin 135, Bureau of American Ethnology. Washington, D.C.: GPO, 1941.

Shoemaker, Edmund C. "Fort Towson: An Early Communications Route to Oklahoma." *Red River Valley Historical Review* 7 (Summer 1982): 18–29.

Sibley, Marilyn McAdams. "The Texas-Cherokee War of 1839." *East Texas Historical Journal* 3 (1965): 18–33.

Smith, Betty Anderson. "Distribution of Eighteenth-Century Cherokee Settlements." In *The Cherokee Indian Nation: A Troubled History,* edited by Duane King. Knoxville, Tenn.: University of Tennessee Press, 1979.

Social Science Research Council. "Acculturation: An Exploratory Formulation." *American Anthropologist* 56 (December 1954): 973–1000.

Strickland, Rex W. "Miller County, Arkansas Territory, the Frontier that Men Forgot." *Chronicles of Oklahoma* 18 (March 1940): 12–34; 18 (June 1940): 154–70; 19 (March 1941): 37–54.

Thornton, Russell. "Cherokee Population Losses During the Trail of Tears: A New Perspective and a New Estimate." *Ethnohistory* 31 (1984): 289–300.

Webb, Clarence. "A Review of Northeast Texas Archeology." *Bulletin 29 of the Texas Archeological Society* (1960): 35–62.

Whitaker, Arthur P. "Spain and the Cherokee Indians." *North Carolina Historical Review* 4 (July 1927): 252–69.
Wilms, Douglas C. "Cherokee Acculturation and Changing Land Use Practices." *Chronicles of Oklahoma* 56 (Fall 1978): 330–43.
Winfrey, Dorman. "Chief Bowles of the Texas Cherokee." *Chronicles of Oklahoma* 32 (Spring 1954): 29–41.
Winkler, Ernest W. "The Cherokee Indians in Texas." *Quarterly of the Texas State Historical Association* 7 (October 1903): 95–165.
Woldert, Albert. "The Last of the Cherokees in Texas and the Life and Death of Chief Bowles." *Chronicles of Oklahoma* 1 (June 1923): 179–226.
Wunder, John R., and Rebecca Herring. "Frontier Conspiracy: Law, History, Turner, and the Cordova Rebellion." *Red River Valley Historical Review* 7 (Summer 1962): 51–67.

Theses and Dissertations

Markman, Robert Paul. "The Arkansas Cherokees: 1817–1828." Ph.D. dissertation, University of Oklahoma, 1972.
Pate, James P. "The Chickamauga: A Forgotten Segment of Indian Resistance on the Southern Frontier." Ph.D. dissertation, Mississippi State University, 1969.

Index